CHINQUA WHERE?

The Spirit of Rural America, 1947-1955

FRED B. McKINLEY

Willow Creek Publishing Company
North Myrtle Beach, SC
2003

Illustrations by Calvin Blassingame

CHINQUA WHERE? The Spirit of Rural America, 1947-1955 /Fred
B. McKinley. p. cm. Includes illustrations; recommended reading and reference list; and index.

ISBN: 0-9729655-0-5

Library of Congress Control Number: 2003103594

1. Chinquapin (TX), Nostalgia of, 1947-1955.
2. San Augustine County (TX), Nostalgia of, 1947-1955—East
    Texas Social History, 1947-1955—Memoirs, 1947-1955.

Willow Creek Publishing Company
North Myrtle Beach, SC 29582
chinquawhere.com

Professional Press
Chapel Hill, NC 27516
USA

To Mom and Dad,

who not only provided the vision
but the means to realize my dreams,

and to Dottie,

who patiently listens.

It has always been the essential process by which man rises from a state of nature, to that of civilization, from darkness to light, from slavery to freedom, that he advances as by the steps of a ladder. This is the method provided by the laws of nature, at times retarded and slow in its operation, but certain to lead to glorious heights if persistently pursued, and devoutly followed.

Grand Lodge of Texas, A.F. & A.M.,
Monitor of the Lodge

Contents

Contents

List of Illustrations

Foreword

In this collection of short essays, Fred McKinley recalls his experiences of growing up in rural East Texas in the late 1940s and early 1950s. For readers who have grown up in the age of air conditioning, television, computers, wireless phones and electronic games, McKinley's picture of life without electricity, indoor plumbing, running water and central heat will be unfamiliar. For older readers it will bring back memories of the simplicity of rural life when baths were taken in a washtub, when boys and girls wore shirts and dresses made from flour sacks and when children went barefoot during the summer months. It was a time when playing with family pets, wandering in the woods, listening to a battery-operated radio and watching Saturday-afternoon movies at the cinema provided the main entertainment.

CHINQUA WHERE?

CHINQUA WHERE? The Spirit of Rural America, 1947-1955 reminds one of the pleasures and disappointments of rural childhood: early attempts at smoking grapevine, the first day of school, cold biscuits and sausage for lunch, puppy love, schoolyard fights, boyhood pranks and attempts to sell Cloverine Salve in order to win a premium that soon broke.

A host of lovable characters pass through the pages of McKinley's narrative: his grandfather Daddy Wright, who extended credit to all his customers at the general store and never received payment from many; parents Fred and Myrtle McKinley who, while struggling to make ends meet, instilled values of honesty and integrity in their son; his buddy Everett Henley who introduced Fred to smoking; Noble Garrett, the community water witcher; cousin Pascal Dickerson, the rodeo performer; friend Hub Christie, who frightened and sometimes cut people with his knife; Carlo de Carlo, the schoolyard bully; Patsy Loggins, the older girl who gave Fred a schoolyard beating; friend Nolan Ainsworth, whose imaginary diseases got Fred into trouble; and Mabel Lois Dickerson, Fred's first girl friend, who taught him the perils of excessive spending on credit.

Readers will be reminded of animals that played a part in their early lives. For Fred it was Nick, the family mule; Joe, the Brahma bull; and Lep, the family dog.

CHINQUA WHERE? recaptures humorous and bitter-sweet memories of a rural life that came to an end when the family barn burned down. Fred's father gave up farming and took a good-paying job at the Evadale Paper Mill north of Beaumont. The family sold the farm and moved to the "big city" of Silsbee, but Fred would never forget those early days in rural East Texas. His warm and moving narrative reminds us of a peaceful and less stress-ful time in our early lives. It is a work that should be read and shared with friends and family.

Ralph A. Wooster

To the Reader

I am told that everyone has a story. Although this is but a part of mine, it is not my purpose to present a formal autobiography or a set of memoirs. I am not that bold. Such works are best left to great statesmen, generals, politicians and other notables who take their contributions far more seriously than I do.

CHINQUA WHERE? The Spirit of Rural America, 1947-1955 is not the standard historical narrative, complete with bibliography and research notes, and it is not a genealogical study of my family. Far from it, as I openly admit in the Prologue. No one from the Chinquapin area, to the best of my knowledge, has ever made the Most Famous List, and no great event of historical record ever took place there.

Now that I've told you what it is not, I will tell you what it is, in terms of intended goals. The premise is simple.

Briefly stated, this book should be read as it was written, through the eyes of a child. It represents a collection of humorous, nostalgic, factual stories and accounts as recalled by a naïve, shy and often mischievous lad, who from the age of four through eleven, had the good fortune to live, breathe and experience the inestimable, colorful, rural and agricultural life of deep East Texas. Each day during the period of 1947 through the early part of 1955 left an indelible mark on my persona in much the same way as rings distinguish the growth of a tree.

Both my parents, and especially my mother, interpreted life, no matter how bright or how dreary, as a series of lessons. Mom continually stressed that for every cause, there is an effect, and to further advance that theory, she interjected old sayings and terminology that would drive home specific points. I have made liberal use of these mechanics in the following pages.

As you know, Texans are known for their drawl. Although attempting to limit its use within the dialogue, I yielded to temptation in a couple of spots by inserting "I'm a-fixin' to" and "up yonder a piece," because without a sampling, no book about Texas would be complete.

CHINQUA WHERE? is geared toward the general reader, but others will determine whether or not, I have achieved that end. Regardless, I propose that all life stories are important in the scheme of time, as a single piece of a puzzle is to the whole, and it is only through this medium that future readers and historians can gain a true insight into the social past.

I am greatly indebted to a longtime mentor, Ralph A. Wooster of Lamar University in Beaumont, the noted Civil War and Texas historian who graciously penned the Foreword to this chronicle. Dr. Wooster provides constant inspiration to associates and peers alike, as well as to his present students and former ones like me who, after attending his military history lectures, claim that they actually heard the cannons roar and the rifles fire, smelled the spent gun powder and witnessed the terrible aftermath of battle.

My heartfelt appreciation also goes to Kenneth Champion, who provided the remarks found on the book's reverse cover. As a highly respected teacher and counselor with the Buna Independent School District, Mr. Champion guided my early and feeble attempts at writing, later, as a colleague, he lent valuable advice on how to best manage a classroom.

I am grateful to James D. Ward, Grand Secretary of the Grand Lodge of Texas, A.F. & A.M., for extending permission to quote both the Introductory Paragraph, along with the one found in the Appendix, directly from the *Monitor of the Lodge*. Masonry has always played an important role in my family whose memberships span generations, and it is my sincere hope that I have honored the craft with references contained herein.

I also want to thank Medtech, Inc., the company that currently produces White Cloverine Salve, and specifically two employees, Cynthia Millard, Consumer Affairs Manager, and Aris DiGiulio, Manager of the Personal Care and First Aid Brands Division, both whom expedited my request and granted approval for the use of the Cloverine name in this publication.

And finally, I tip my hat to Dottie, my beloved wife, who spent hours putting ideas about the illustrations onto rough sketches which the talented Calvin Blassingame used to base the final results.

As a matter of clarification, all communities, towns, cities, counties and other geographical entities included in this work are assumed to be located in Texas, unless otherwise specified.

At the onset, I apologize to those family members, friends and neighbors who failed to receive honorable mention. Though not named, these individuals contributed greatly, and without them, life would have certainly taken a much different course. Furthermore, if I have misrepresented names, dates and events, or hurt the feelings of anyone, I did so unintentionally. A lot of water has flowed under the proverbial bridge since the mid-1950s.

As one of my friends so aptly put it, "No matter how

short, I'm just happy to have a memory left after all these years."

That is a true statement, if I ever heard one.

Fred B. McKinley

Prologue

The Spirit of Americana

I have always held a strong sense of and relationship to the past. As a child, I asked my grandparents, almost ad nauseam, to tell me about our genealogy. As I grew, so did my keen interest in history and family matters. I sought to understand where my lineage began, and I asked them specifically to identify the wars in which my forefathers fought.

These questions were fueled by beautiful pictures displayed on calendars, provided free by the local merchants and passed out as advertisements. I recall one calendar in particular that dealt with military history. Each month contained a different scene pitting opposing forces in a hotly contested action that made my imagination run wild. My two favorites were the lithographs depicting the Battle of Bunker Hill during the American Revolution and the Confederate advance on Little Round Top as the American Civil War raged on at the small Pennsylvania town of Gettysburg.

Each morning while munching on Post Toasties, I gazed at the illustrations and concluded that some of my ancestors must have participated in at least one of these engagements. I sincerely believed that it would be just a matter of time before I had hard evidence to document the theory. The queries, unfortunately, were never answered to my satisfaction, and the proof never presented itself. After swallowing that bitter pill, I wrestled with the fact that none of the older family members knew anything about their grandparents, not even their names.

How can this be? I thought. No matter how hard I tried to rationalize the issue, I failed to grasp how it was possible that my own grandparents could never get beyond one generation in their respective family trees. Many nights I lay awake pondering these serious concerns—fleshing out plans to give my departed forebears a stern talking to when I met them in the Great Beyond, providing of course that all of them, including me, made it to the same destination.

As a four-year-old, I held them personally responsible for negligence. After all, they had not ensured that future generations would be knowledgeable about the family roots. They should have seen to it that such important information was not only written down, but kept up to date.

Later in life, when I became interested in sports, I drew a comparison between the duties of a family historian and that of a wide receiver on any football team. I speculated that my kin plainly dropped the ball, so to speak, and in a broad sense, they should have paid more attention to details.

I remain convinced that many share these same sentiments and common experiences, along with another haunting scenario. At one time or another, all of us have wandered from the interstate highways or major thoroughfares and passed through a little village or community. The reasons vary. Maybe we wanted to view the local scenery or eat and rest a while. Perhaps we were just running low on fuel and needed to fill up. On other occasions, we may have taken a wrong turn and found ourselves on some back road, hoping to find an easy way back to civilization, as we like to call it. If the husband happened to be behind the wheel that day, however, there would have been plenty of time for sightseeing. Despite arguments to the contrary, most men never stop and seek directions. Ask any wife—she will attest to that!

After observing a deserted farmhouse standing in the middle of some field or overgrown pasture, we become puzzled. So we turn to our fellow passengers and pose insightful questions such as: "I wonder who lived there over the years?" or "If walls could talk, what would they say? What stories could they tell?" These familiar expressions have been permanently etched into the American vocabulary, and I would venture to say that each of us either hear or use them almost on a daily basis.

Other times, we may stop at a traffic signal and see a house on the right or upon the left that during its day stood as a beacon in the community. Admittedly, some of these sightings have appeared strangely familiar to me, even though I had never before set foot in that part of the country. But I suppose that small towns and hamlets are much the same and that would explain away the sometimes-eerie stirrings at the base of the neck—those little tingles—which you may have felt during a similar encounter?

Whether tourists or passers-by, we nod our heads, then continue on our way. Attempts at further research usually provide more frustration. Few answers are brought to light, because very little is written. We fail to understand because of a very simple logic—the lack of publicity. Either no famous person was born near there, or no outstanding event, even if it did occur, was ever recorded. Most of the past is known only by a handful of local folks, and once the older generation moves on or dies out, so do their stories. Therein lies the real irony.

We should and must remember that these minuscule and sometimes now extinct areas are clearly as important as sprawling metropolitan cities, because they too produced citizens who were the salt of the earth. Your past generations and mine, whether teachers, ranchers, grocers, farmers, wives, overseers, small businessmen or others of any vocation, all contributed to the growth of their respective communities, states and to this great nation. Each individual exhibited considerable merit in his or her own way, with collective dreams and desires.

But in the end, most of their goals were too lofty and therefore remained unattainable. Formal instruction beyond high school, and ofttimes the elementary level, was rare. In many cases, even that yielded to the pressures placed on an agrarian society and forced many youngsters, both male and female, to leave the classroom during their early school years. While many of our ancestors never obtained basic learning skills and could neither read nor write, they were extremely intelligent, because these folks received their education at one of the two great institutions of higher learning: the School of Hard Knocks and the University of Life.

So it is with Chinquapin. You ask, "Where is it?" or "What the heck is Chinquapin?"

Your questions are no different than most, because when people inquire about my childhood home, I proudly proclaim that I'm from Chinquapin. That summons a response that rarely ever changes, "Chinqua where?"

Return with me if you will to a more innocent time and place. Although the stories recounted on the following pages took place in deep Southeast Texas during the period of 1947 through early 1955, the events could have occurred anywhere in rural Americana during that era.

Recollections of growing up are timeless. Anyone who has ever lived in small-town America should be able to identify with the Everett Henleys; the Dickerson girls; first pets and first loves; small-town sheriffs; city marshals who toted pearl-handled revolvers; the Hub Christies, who were misunderstood by most except innocent children; small schools and bullies; and the day-to-day problems associated with trying to make it in the farming business from one season to the other without going bankrupt. Some should be able to remember the times before fast-paced living, modern appliances, televisions and personal computers placed unrelenting stresses on the family unit.

These stories are equally dedicated to the past, present and future—and to the patriotic flame best described as the *Spirit of Americana*. For those who yearn to relive some of the so-called "good old days," or those who wish to experience them for the first time, hopefully the following will allow that small window of opportunity. If in the reading process, one pauses to wipe a little mist from one's eyes, maybe chuckles a bit, perhaps reflects briefly on a comparable circumstance or remembers a loved one, I have achieved some measure of success.

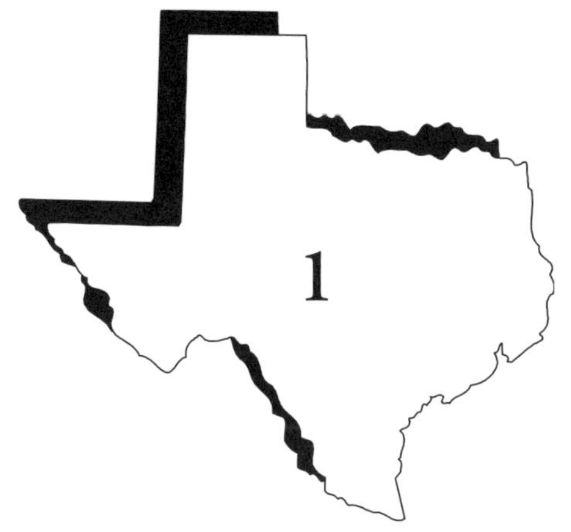

CHINQUA WHERE?

ESTLED AMONG THE SOUTHEAST TEXAS PINES just off State Highway 96 and near the intersections of State Highway 103 and FM 1751 between San Augustine and Bronson, lies a small community named Chinquapin (pronounced chink-a-pin). Don't bother consulting the road atlas, because the community does not appear on contemporary maps. There are no signs to welcome you, and if you get lost, don't expect to see any named streets. In fact, few people other than old-timers or current residents of San Augustine County know anything about its past.

No one is quite sure where that name *Chinquapin* came from, as local historians and others who have written about it rarely agree on the subject. Over the years, however, I have encountered numerous "bullosophers" who were most generous with their opinions. For those of you who've never heard of a bullosopher, it is this East Texan's way of describing a homespun philosopher who stretches the truth a bit, but not enough to hurt anything.

While some expounded the hypothesis that the designation of Chinquapin originated with a local Indian tribe, others claim that it is the namesake of the small nut found within the burr of the chinquapin tree. I have it on good authority from Don C. Marler's work, *Fort Terán on the Neches River*, that most of this tree type, only six to eight inches in diameter when fully grown, are gone now, succumbing to disease, blight and "modern timber-cutting practices." Adding to the confusion, there is another indigenous category referred to as the chinquapin oak, which is related to the chestnut, but is almost extinct, having been killed by an imported Chinese cricket.

But let's return to the discussion about the origin of the name Chinquapin. I always believed that it is derived from the mighty Chinquapin Creek, also known as Egg Nog Branch (all of fifteen feet wide and a little more than ten miles long), which flows between its borders toward the Ayish Bayou. As for Chinquapin Creek, I'll leave it for others to argue the point of how it got its identity. I do, however, have an idea. Perhaps the creek once brimmed with the variety of fish known as chinquapin, similar and often confused in other regions of the country with white perch and crappie, pronounced both krap-e and krop-

e. In parts of neighboring Louisiana, as you might have guessed, they are correctly called chinquapin. (If you were wondering about that Egg Nog Branch thing, I wouldn't touch that with a ten-foot pole.) There seems to be a lot of conflicting information and uncertainty here, so we will move on.

Now before we go too far, let me explain that in its heyday, according to the *Texas Almanac* and a few landmarks—but mostly by way of common knowledge—Chinquapin, Texas sported a thriving population of about a hundred folks, scores of coon dogs and foxhounds, two general stores, several sawmills and a multitude of one-horse power plants that produced syrup from sugar cane and sorghum. There was also a cotton gin that had been torn down long before I was born. However, I played on the remaining foundation, marveled at the sights of the rusted machinery that had been left behind, and imagined what it must have been like to live in Chinquapin when the Industrial Revolution, although extremely limited, finally caught up with this remote part of Texas.

My maternal grandfather, Lloyd Napoleon "Pony" Wright, operated one of the general stores. Daddy Wright, as the grandchildren called him, was one of the kindest and most freehearted men I ever knew, and I always credited him with inventing and applying the concept of the Easy Payment Plan years before Sears & Roebuck used it to build their merchandising empire. He extended credit to numerous heads of households, and single-handedly, I am told, placed more store-bought groceries on the tables of that community than any other person in his time.

He entered those purchases inside huge ledger books beside the names of friends and neighbors who promised to pay as soon as they could, or when their crops came in. Most, I might add, never did for one reason or the other, but that really didn't matter in the long run.

At various stages, he owned several store buildings in Chinquapin. Once a fire completely destroyed all of the contents, including the books that we refer to today as accounts receivable. I asked him how he proved to people what they owed, and whether he ever got his money. He said that of all the people who "were into him" for literally hundreds of dollars, only one stepped forward and paid his obligation in full. When I inquired whether these same deadbeats asked for future credit, Daddy Wright replied that he never held a grudge. To my astonishment, he said that he allowed them to "beat" him time and again. Moreover, innocent wives and children might go to bed hungry if he took the hard-line approach and adopted the cash-and-carry mentality. He just couldn't say no and turn away those in need.

Besides the industry that I described earlier, farming represented the main means of support, and when I allude to that term, I mean poor dirt farmers, the ones who walked behind a plow and a team of mules from daylight to dusk.

Modern technology was almost nonexistent in the community even by 1949, the year that I started school. Few cars were found on the narrow one-lane dirt roads that turned muddy and almost impassable when the rains came. The school system, constantly strapped for cash, owned but one battle-scarred yellow bus that picked up all of the children, about sixty or seventy and carried them to the three-room schoolhouse on land that my great-grandfather, Jesse Miles Drawhorn, and my uncle, George Lewis, had owned and donated to the community.

The original schoolhouse, where my parents, Fred and Myrtle Wright McKinley, attended as children and where my mother taught, had been destroyed by fire years earlier. Its replacement—the one that I remember—came in the form of a giant structure that sported three huge classrooms and an auditorium where cakewalks and other community social activities were held. It also contained a massive lunchroom where cooks like Grace Dickerson and Lucy Sharp Lewis served up those horrendous vittles that included the likes of dried black-eyed peas, lima beans, cornbread—and the worst of them all—that dreaded hominy. Even today, I shy away from most of these foods.

Chinquapin had two houses of worship, both Baptist. My grandfathers, John McKinley and Pony Wright, were deacons in the same church, and although both men were unusually headstrong, they learned to tolerate each other, at least for a while. The original building, long since gone prior to 1947 and replaced by a second, served also as the meeting place for the local Pentecostals. So it was not unheard of for folks of one denomination to attend the religious services of the other.

This practice, however, did not sit well with many Baptist members, and in fact once, Grandpa McKinley's own half-brother and his wife, Louis Van Schoubroek and Fannie Ainsworth, were turned out of the church, because they were found guilty of such wayward conduct. Later, after careful reexamination, the elders allowed the couple to return to the fold.

Daddy Wright went down the road a mile or so toward Bronson and founded Pine Grove Baptist Church, after being expelled from the first when he and Grandpa McKinley failed to resolve a controversy over whether a piano should be used to accompany the congregational singing. Even though Grandpa McKinley won the day with his pro-piano views, Mom got the last word in the quarrel, because she bought the windows for Daddy Wright's new church. I learned very early in life about the effects of heated religious arguments. You know how we Baptists are when it comes to internal bickering!

Chinquapin, however, represented more than a mere location or a flyspeck on old Texas maps. It contained a special spirit that represented *Americana*. Although primitive conditions existed in every corner as late as 1955, most citizens with their meager incomes lived far better than previous generations.

The majority of families had been touched by World War II, sending either fathers or sons to fight and die for their country as their ancestors had done countless times before them. My paternal grandparents, John and Lizzie McKinley, sent all three sons and all three came back. Uncle George and Aunt Laura Lewis were not as lucky. Corporal John D. Lewis lost his life in Belgium on September 6, 1944.

The folks' background lay in Scots-Irish ancestry and in those who migrated from Virginia, the Carolinas, Tennessee, Georgia, Alabama, Mississippi and Louisiana. These people remembered their grandparents' recollections of the Civil War and its terrible aftereffects. The depths of the Great Depression remained fresh in everyone's mind, and a lingering mistrust of banks prevailed. It was the time of Truman, "I like Ike," staunch conservatism and social naïveté.

CHINQUA WHERE?

The residents of Chinquapin aligned closely with the county seat, located about eight miles away. Referred to as the Cradle of Texas, San Augustine was founded about 1716 by Spanish missionaries who built the Mission Nuestra Señora de los Delores on the banks of the Ayish Bayou. The town that grew around the mission incorporated by 1834, greatly contributed toward Texas independence and figured prominently in the founding of the Republic.

Early on, I read accounts that placed Davy Crockett right smack dab in the middle of San Augustine County on his way to San Antonio and the ill-fated battle at the Alamo. Many times I walked through our pastures and wondered perhaps if I trod in the steps of the Tennessee legend. The thought sent shivers down my spine. Numerous reports also mentioned that Sam Houston visited San Augustine frequently. When I walked those hallowed streets, again I imagined the Father of Texas standing beside me and discussing the old days at San Jacinto, when he captured General Antonio López de Santa Anna and sent the Mexican army skedaddling back to Mexico.

I grew up alongside another Texas giant, James Pinckney Henderson. Well, not really. Although he passed away in 1858, I always remembered seeing the massive statue of the first governor of Texas perched at the front entrance of the San Augustine Courthouse.

DAVY CROCKETT
JAMES PINCKNEY HENDERSON
SAM HOUSTON
COUNTRY MUSINGS
CALVIN BLASSINGAME

CHINQUA WHERE?

Dad often talked about Ben Ramsey, another color-ful, contemporary Texas political figure. He boasted that he not only knew the lieutenant governor personally, but he also played poker with him on several occasions. He added that Ben loved cards and good sipping whiskey.

So it would be safe to say that San Augustine's past, both town and county, had an enormous impact on my upbringing, as with numerous others. Anne Clark pretty well summed up the contribution when she wrote in *Historic Homes of San Augustine*:

> Through the years San Augustine has furnished many notable men in the civil, military, and judicial ranks of the state, including one president, one vice-president, three governors, two lieutenant governors, one Confederate States congressman, three judges of the Supreme Court, six district judges, two generals in the Texas Army and four generals in the Confederate Army.

My family first settled in the Chinquapin area about March 1839. But when I arrived in 1947 when my parents moved from Beaumont, many conditions had changed little. Our home sported neither electricity, running water, inside plumbing nor any of the modern conveniences taken for granted in nearby San Augustine, which was also well known for its superior architecture.

Even so, our household laid claim to a few luxuries. The family "watched" the battery-operated radio every Saturday night and listened to the Grand Ole Opry, where stars, including Roy Acuff, Hank Williams, Hank Snow, Ernest Tubb and Kitty Wells, took center stage. Some of the saddest occasions occurred when our radio battery went dead during the broadcasts, and we had to go to bed without hearing the rest of the scheduled performances. But nothing ever compared to the pall cast on the program that followed January 1, 1953, the day that Hank Williams died.

We also owned an old tattered icebox and took weekly deliveries of fifty-pound blocks of ice that we fought to keep from melting. In youthful ignorance, I called ice "fifty," and it was not until the age of five that I knew any better.

But as with every coin, two sides exist. We dealt with outright poverty on a daily basis, and currency was as scarce as hens' teeth. I recall at least twice when Mom sent me pedaling on my bicycle for two miles to the local general store with orders to purchase a gallon of milk. At some point or another each year, the milk cow on which we depended went dry, and we resorted to buying the product or doing without. On those two particular occasions, Mom admonished me to protect the dollar bill as if my life depended on it. She'd say, "This is the last one we have to our name, so you'd better not lose it!"

At the time, however, I really didn't dwell on our wretched state of negative cash flow. It became unimportant, because most every member of that local community shared the same circumstances. We were all extremely poor, but didn't realize it. Or at least, that's the way it seemed.

We never owned an outhouse either. "Wow!" you say and then ask, "Where did you go to the bathroom?" In the country way back then, one had to improvise. No matter how severe the weather conditions, we took care of business behind the barn or out in the woods. Very early, I became familiar—up close and personal, you might say—with pages torn from the Ward's or Sears' mail order catalogues, large tree leaves and those awful, rough corncobs. I'll leave the rest for your imagination.

Once I asked my dad why he didn't build an outhouse for us. I explained that Grandpa and Grandma McKinley had one, and so did most of our neighbors. Because my grandparents possessed one of those two-holer privies, I always felt that they were extremely well off. Dad replied that he would eventually get around to building one for us, but he never found the time or the "round tuit." Years later, I questioned Mom about this situation. Quick on the defense, she pointed out that Dad didn't have a lazy bone in his body; he just did not want to bother with the facility's maintenance. I suppose that he had a good point!

Since electricity had not yet come to this neck of the woods, we used kerosene lamps and lanterns until June 1949 when the Rural Electrification Agency (REA) turned on the lights. Later I reminisced that I could have boasted of starting school and getting-up my lessons by lamplight if power had been supplied a mere three months later. Old Abe Lincoln and I almost had a lot in common.

Times and conditions were harsh, and I suppose that in many ways we lived as those in medieval times. Even so, things were evolving quickly, but through a child's eyes, however, the world continued to move at a snail's pace.

*It is fortunate to come of distinguished ancestry.
It is not less so to be such that people do not care to
inquire whether you are of high descent or not.*

—Jean La Bruyere

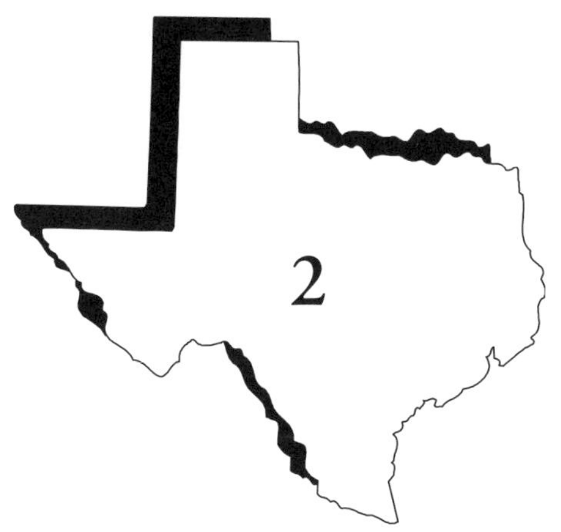

ARMADILLOS AND TOBACCO DON'T MIX

BOTH MY MOTHER AND FATHER SMOKED CIGArettes, as did most of our family friends and neighbors. Dad preferred to roll his own; perhaps it was much cheaper that way. He always kept a carton or two of Prince Albert tobacco stashed away in his bedroom. What I didn't realize then, but learned to my regret later on, was that Mom kept a mental count of the number of cans on hand at any given moment.

My buddy, Everett Henley, who was about ten years old, had been smoking, or at least he claimed that he had, for quite a while. By slipping around behind his barn and out in the woods whenever he had the urge to light up, he had been able to keep his habit under close wraps. His parents, Truitt and Rosa, were never the wiser. But

Everett let me in on his little secret, and I personally witnessed and marveled at the way he was able to place loose tobacco in a paper, roll it around, then lick and seal it in a mechanical and almost flawless effort. To the untrained eye, the finished product looked like a store-bought cigarette! So I suppose it was inevitable that I yield to temptation.

During the summers Everett and I played a lot together. He was nearer my age than any of our closest neighbors—if you can call two miles close. I would cut across our pasture and through the woods to his house in no time flat, especially when our Brahma bull, Joe, felt mean and wanted to give chase to anything or anyone who dared enter his territory. Everett and I spent many a lazy summer day swimming in a creek near his house, exploring the forests, hunting squirrels, birds and rabbits—generally goofing off. Of course, when I left home to join Everett on these outings, Mom always wanted to know what my plans were and who I was going with.

I usually replied, "Everett and I are going to mess around." Such lingo, in that day and age, covered the entire spectrum of events in a youngster's daily life, both planned and actual.

One day we were in the woods as usual. Everett stopped at a tree and pulled a large grapevine from one of the limbs. He crumbled some of the bark into his hand, then reached inside one of his pockets, pulled out some cigarette papers and proceeded to roll a smoke. He asked if I wanted to participate, and when I said I did, he handed the paraphernalia my way. Being the novice, I spent the next several minutes fumbling around until Everett finally took pity on my futile attempt and came to my aid.

If you've never experienced smoking grapevine—and for the life of me, I could never understand why I or anyone else would—you can't imagine how hot it is to your tongue and mouth. After several draws, I told Everett that this blend just wasn't going to be my smoke of choice, and furthermore, I couldn't deal with the pain.

"What about regular tobacco?" he asked.

"I'm not sure," I replied. "Is it any better than what we've been smoking?"

My friend responded by producing a pouch of Bugler, and we proceeded to roll one of those. Much to my surprise, it did represent a vast improvement over what I had just endured.

Now it's hard to explain just what fascination smoking held for me, especially when you consider that I was only nine years old. Regardless of age, however, the spree began, and over the next few months, it changed my life forever. Everett and I used Bugler or Prince Albert, and occasionally we even saved enough cash to spring for some "ready rolls," the term we affectionately placed on store-bought brands such as Camels, Chesterfields and Kools. I never knew where Everett got those cigarettes, whether purchased by others or whatever, but he always seemed to have a steady source. Perhaps his parents unknowingly supplied them.

One day I let it slip that Dad had some Prince Albert at our house, so Everett suggested that I requisition a can or two but not enough to arouse suspicion. I followed through on that idea, and for a while at least, everything went according to the master blueprint.

When at my house, Everett and I smoked in secure areas. It's a small wonder that we never caused a forest fire or burned down the barn along with all adjacent structures, but I suppose that someone with far greater powers looked out for us. But danger took many forms. Transporting the cache became too much of an ordeal, because once, Mom almost questioned the huge bulge in my front pocket. We dared not let my parents find out about the recent activity, so we had to be extra-careful. Fearing detection and certain punishment, Everett and I made a fateful decision to keep a full complement of tobacco, papers and matches at two sites, retaining the original at his house but establishing a newer one at mine.

I seriously considered where I should plant my stockpile. I couldn't keep it in my room, because Mother would surely find it—you know how mothers are about those things. After careful and thorough deliberation, I concluded that I should store it somewhere in or around the barn. That was the best and safest place, but exactly where? This question gave me fits, until I finally decided upon a foolproof plan. I cut a plank out of the back inside wall that led into the hay bin, installed some rubber hinges made from a used tire, and inserted my smoking supplies where they would surely remain safe from all harm and inquiring minds. With the construction project completed, I felt a little smug.

"Everett," I proudly stated, "there's nothing to worry about on this end. This 'vault' is just as good as Fort Knox." He nodded in agreement.

Dad had recently attended a veteran's educational course on woodworking, which was taught at the Burleson schoolhouse. For his final assignment and as a present to me, he built a large student desk, which we placed proudly in the living room. Each day when I arrived from school, I stored my books inside the large, top middle drawer until snacks and playtime concluded and I had to attend to homework.

One particular afternoon, my life changed drastically. As I entered the front door and greeted my parents, I noticed that both seemed unusually somber. They were seated like mannequins, stiff as a board and glaring in my direction. I thought at first that some member of the family had died, because I couldn't recall a time when either of them ever sat down at four o'clock in the afternoon to welcome me home from a hard day at school. Something was really wrong, but what?

I didn't have to wait long to find out. When I opened the desk drawer, I thought that my eyes were playing tricks on me, because tobacco, paper and matches— all strangely familiar—were right there before me. My heart beat as never before, and I came pretty close at nine years old to having a myocardial infarction. In considerable shock and disbelief, I threw my books on top of the goods, shut the drawer as fast as possible, then turned to my parents and announced that I had to take care of other duties. Somehow, deep down, I knew that I would never make it to the door, a scant five feet away, much less to the outside world and safety.

Was I right! Dad stopped me in mid-stride. In a peculiar voice he asked, "Don't you want a smoke before you go?"

Immediately, two things began to puzzle me. The first mystery was how in the world had my cigarette material got inside the desk when it was supposed to be tucked away safely in the secret hiding place in the barn? I had been extremely cautious when I put it there, picking a time when both Mom and Dad were busy working in the fields. I knew that Everett would never squeal on a pal, yet here it was in full view. The second issue, which posed an even greater threat, was how should I deal with the dilemma? So far, Dad had remained relatively calm given the situation, and for him this was totally uncharacteristic.

I turned to reply and muttered, "No, much obliged. I don't think that I would care for a cigarette right now. Maybe later on, after supper."

In a vain and gallant effort to circumvent the subject, I asked permission to leave the room, but this was not to be, not yet anyway. I was told in no uncertain terms to sit on the sofa and stand ready to answer some serious questions truthfully.

In throwing myself on the mercy of what seemed to be a new Spanish Inquisition, I explained that all the stuff did belong to me. I promised to never smoke again, if only they let me off with good behavior. Please understand that my parents never abused me, but I was knowledgeable about the sting inflicted by a peach-tree switch or a razor strap on my bottom side. This was, however, the first time that I ever considered myself in deep, deep trouble, and I was totally unprepared for the eventual outcome.

My father responded with a half-smile. Today, as I look back on the experience, he must have been remembering a similar occasion when his father held an identical conversation with him.

He said, "Son, we're not going to punish you, but we do have some issues to iron out. The only thing that we ask in return is that you tell the truth."

I was dumbfounded! My father had never, to the best of my knowledge, subscribed to the art of psychology, especially when it came to a reprimand. His prevailing policy leaned more in the direction of a belt to the backside. I began to feel guilty, and more so when I glanced toward my mother and saw tears well up in those kind eyes. She appeared as though she would start crying at any second.

Dad continued the stern lecture about the dangers of smoking at such a young age and how it would slow one's growth. He expressed personal disappointment and challenged me to think about the hidden perils. What would have happened if I had set the barn on fire? He concluded that if I wanted to smoke and felt big enough for the test, I should do it openly, without shame. Never mind that most people would label them as terrible parents—there was no need to sneak around. Dad began to lay it on thick! He mentioned that in all his years he had never seen or heard tell of a nine-year-old boy walking around San Augustine County with a cigarette dangling from the corner of his mouth.

When I responded that Everett had more than likely, Dad said, "Hush, I'll do all the talking for now. You just sit there and listen. I'm making a point here!" He added that I may have set some type of record with my latest stunt. (He really liked that word *stunt,* and used it as often as he could to describe my various forms of mischief.)

I honestly tried to pay strict attention and act like I understood this massive verbal barrage, but when he got to the part about how a real man has a duty to guard his legacy, my eyes glazed over. All of this jargon left me completely confused. At one time I thought that my first puff of a cigarette had given me the sickest feeling yet, but nothing could compare to this salvo.

Mom was relatively quiet until she blurted out, "Fred Barry, just how long have you been smoking anyway?"

Without thinking properly, I responded, "Oh, not long. Why?"

"Well," Mom remarked, "surely long enough to go through about half a carton of Prince Albert."

It finally dawned on me that I should confess to all and admit that Everett and I had taken a number of cans. So I did. Mom, however, was not yet ready to move on, forgive—or forget. She added that they would have let me off much sooner if I had come clean from the onset. That should have provided me with the earliest clue about future dealings with the opposite sex.

Oh boy, I thought, *now she tells me. Surely this is another one of those lessons learned a little too late.*

After an hour or so of grilling by what seemed akin to Gestapo tactics, I began to presume that I had gotten through this mess without appreciable damage. Finally I gathered enough courage to ask, "How did you find it?"

Dad stated that while he was "taking a morning walk" behind the barn, the evidence lay in plain sight. Perhaps an armadillo was responsible.

I remarked to myself, "Oh, no! Not one of those varmints!"

For all of you non-native Texans who don't realize that armadillos are as basic to that state as fleas are to dogs, I will explain exactly what they are good for. Nothing, absolutely nothing! Armadillos are a nuisance, to say the least, to farmers and to just about anyone I can possibly think of. While searching and rummaging for insects, they pillage, loot and destroy cash crops and vegetable gardens, not to mention flowerbeds and lawns. Now, other things could be added to the list.

For some reason or another, and only God knows for sure, one of those creatures likely had found his way into our barnyard the previous night. He rooted out my tobacco, matches and papers and left everything completely exposed for Dad to find. I might have fared better with Mom if she happened by, but talking my way out of

OH, NO! NOT AN ARMADILLO!
PRINCE ALBERT
CALVIN BLASSINGAME

this one would require a momentous effort. With his verbal engine firing like a Gatling gun on a defenseless buffalo herd, Dad seemed to have a field day with my misfortune; apparently he had nothing better to do than taunt me! With my question finally answered, I expressed that I had learned a valuable lesson that day. Everett would just have to find another smoking buddy.

Forgiveness from my parents came slowly, however, because unfinished business remained. Dad wanted to see me roll a cigarette, light it up and smoke it, and—imagine this—right there in front of Mom, who was still visibly shaken by the cataclysmic event.

I attempted to carry this thing off, and in fact I did rather well, given the circumstance. Painstakingly, I rolled a cigarette, put it in my mouth, lit up as always, and for a brief instant felt as big as any man. Although Dad appeared reasonably impressed by my expertise, Mom was not! When she looked directly at me and commented that I should really be proud of my latest accomplishment, somehow the joy floated away. I put out the cigarette and received the long awaited and overdue permission to go outside and play.

Dad offered one parting bit of advice: "Son, always remember that it's no sin to make a mistake. The real shame is learning nothing from it."

As I nervously walked out of the door, I heard Mom tell Dad, "At least I know now what happened to all that missing tobacco. I blamed you for smoking it without telling me." *At least*, I thought, *I got Dad off the hook on this one.*

From then until much, much later, I never smoked another cigarette. To paraphrase a familiar song made popular by blues singer, B. B. King, the thrill was gone. I also immediately curtailed my practice of hunting squirrels, birds and rabbits. Armadillos became my primary target!

You cannot create experience. You must undergo it.

—Albert Camus

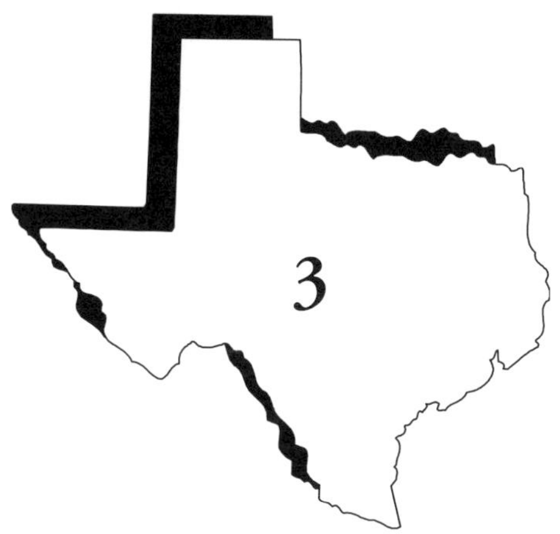

SCHOOLHOUSE BLUES

THIS WASN'T THE ONLY TIME THAT I HAD GOTTEN into hot water because of smoking. Long before Dad found my tobacco and supplies, Everett and I, overconfident by not being discovered, thought it a pretty good idea to partake of an occasional smoke on the school campus. What could be the harm in that?

Our principal, Mr. Nix, a soft-spoken, gray-haired gentleman of slight build, had taught school for a number of years. There was never any doubt that as an authoritative figure, he was a member of the old teachers' corps. As such, he both demanded and received strict discipline in his school. We never knew much about his personal life, except that his daughter had been tragically killed when a steel filing cabinet fell on her. Details of that unfortunate incident were kept, as expected, close to the vest.

CHINQUA WHERE?

Although friendly enough, at least for a principal, Mr. Nix displayed an enigmatic side in that he always wore a dark brown glove on his left hand. This was indeed strange, we thought, because we never saw him take it off. Some of the guys theorized that it must have served as a cover for some awful grisly burn, or maybe a war wound. Others proposed that it masked a false hand of some sort. At one time we sought out a volunteer who would ask him directly, but no one dared to accept the challenge. Mr. Nix served Chinquapin school for two years, during which we were never able to solve the mystery.

Up to that point in my school career, I was never spanked, paddled or whipped, as we liked to call it, in spite of the numerous occasions when I surely deserved it. My parents always warned that if I got a paddling at school, I should expect the same warm reception at home. To me, that represented a pretty good deterrent.

In that very different day and age, teachers seemed to garner more respect than they do at present. Parents rarely questioned motives when they meted out punishment for those unpardonable crimes such as talking in class, chewing gum, fighting, and for God's sake, smoking on the hallowed school grounds. Few held little sympathy for children who came home carrying tales of mistreatment by teachers. These dedicated professionals were merely doing their jobs the best way that they knew how.

One day when the bus stopped at the front drive of the school, I ran immediately to the outhouse, located in a remote section of the campus. By the time my business had been concluded and I was about to report for duty, either Everett, Lee Allen Dickerson, or one of the other five or six of us who congregated there swapping yarns, screamed that Mr. Nix was coming. When I rounded the door, I saw that imposing figure bearing down on us, yelling something about being late for class. He was tired of warning us. Now it was time for action!

Please realize that the Chinquapin version of a tardy signal took an unusual form. A teacher, or student in some cases, would grip a small hand-held bell, stand at the entrance of the building—which I might add was a long way from the outhouse—and ring it like the devil for what seemed about five minutes. The sound of the bell brought all playground functions to an immediate halt. Like little soldiers, children lined up at the front door by grades and then proceeded in quiet, orderly fashion to one of the three classrooms. At least that's the way it was supposed to go.

That particular day, I didn't hear the bell, I swear! But pathetic excuses didn't matter to Mr. Nix, who swung the paddle at every boy who ran past him. His accuracy amazed me. Each felt the sting, including yours truly, who flinched not so much from pain but because that was the first lick of corporal punishment in my school career. What I feared most, however, was that word of this milestone would make its way home to my parents. I was lucky; it didn't.

Even this experience did not deter Everett and me from concocting a plan for continued smoking enjoyment. A huge room, which served as a storage area for worn-out desks and other items, was located to the side of the stage in the auditorium. Everett and I, along with Lee Allen and Nolan Ainsworth, asked for and received Mr. Nix's permission to use that chamber for the purpose of eating our lunches brought from home.

Each of us had decided that our lives would be cut short if we continued to nibble at the food prepared by the school cook. There is just so much a person can stand when it comes to consuming black-eyed peas, lima beans, cornbread and hominy. Besides, this gave us a wonderful opportunity to light up after lunch, and no one would ever find out. For safety precautions, we even installed an inside lock on the door that we assumed would ward away unexpected cowans and eavesdroppers.

Again fate dealt a cruel hand, and the two-edged sword of justice cut deep. We failed to consider that Mr. Nix might be two steps ahead of us.

The national pastime, at least according to Chinquapin standards, was softball. We played every spare moment before and after classes and while waiting for the bus, which usually ran late. During that time of innocence and laxness in a small community, we experienced the thrills of visiting nearby schools, either Broaddus, Burleson or Norwood, almost every Friday afternoon, weather permitting, from 12:30 until it was time to go home. On those days, the driver arrived early and transported the entire student body, along with the principal and two teachers, to the other campuses. At different times, of course, the neighbors reciprocated. Lookouts, posted at the windows, sounded the alarm and heralded the first sighting of another school's bus chugging up the road with a bunch of rowdy kids primed and ready to take on the local competition or spend the allotted time involved in other forms of amusement. We all looked forward to those Fridays and softball games, as they represented a unique way of life steeped in lengthy tradition. However, the day that Mr. Nix knocked on the door of our eating and smoking establishment, combined with the events that followed, radically changed this local flavoring and rendition of Camelot.

Nolan, Lee Allen, Everett and I had just finished eating and lit up. We were having a great time, until the sound of Mr. Nix's cold voice interrupted our parlor party.

"Open the door, boys! I know that you're smoking in there."

Before we complied, all of us were busier than a three-legged hound on a rabbit chase, trying to put out our cigarettes. We placed the butts—some still smoldering—in our lunch boxes and frantically waved our arms and hands in a vain effort to clear away the smoke.

We opened the door sheepishly, and as Mr. Nix entered, stone silence fell. He finally broke the calm with the expected criticism that carried the usual themes of disappointment, honesty and respect for teachers and school property. We felt that the pronouncement of sentence, for which we were all judged guilty beyond reasonable doubt, would surely take the form of a good stiff paddling. But we guessed incorrectly. Mr. Nix stated that he would have to think long and hard about the penalty phase, but for now the room that he had so graciously allowed us to use was off limits. We had broken the trust!

As time wore on, he kept us on edge, never knowing when and how the punishment would be administered. The waiting was the worse part! Then one day Mr. Nix called us to his desk individually. He added to the confusion by asking our opinions on the matter. To a man, we four concluded that he held the trump card; if we relapsed, he could always tell our parents. That was more than enough, we thought, so with a mere apology and

KNOCK!
KNOCK!
YIKES! IT'S MR. NIX!
CALVIN BLASSINGAME

further promise to never again smoke on school property, we should be released on our own recognizance.

Somehow Mr. Nix felt that stronger measures were required. He countered with a proposal that each of us write five hundred times that we would never repeat these atrocious deeds. Furthermore, he agreed to withhold all details from our parents if we complied. What a relief!

There was, however, an addendum to this conference, one that we failed to understand the true impact of until a few days later. Mr. Nix determined that until further notice, everyone in the school would not be allowed to participate in the Friday-afternoon softball frivolities. One and all shared the punishment! He followed up that ruling with announcements to the three classrooms and afterward with letters to the neighboring schools. He stated candidly that he had caught four students, all baseball players, smoking.

Of course, the guilty parties were crushed by the severity of so much castigation. But one thing for sure—Mr. Nix got our attention! At such a young age, the infamous four had never experienced what some now refer to as peer pressure or what I call flat-out ostracism. Everett, Nolan, Lee Allen and I were about to learn the cold hard facts and true meaning of group anger amassed by the entire student body. Even though Mr. Nix never revealed our identities, it didn't take long for everyone to figure out who the culprits were who had caused the grievous harm.

It was a good thing that the four of us liked each other, because we were all that we had. None of the other students spoke to us, and even the teachers and Estes Birdwell, the bus driver, resented our actions. They also enjoyed those outings, and we had taken all that away with a simple puff of a cigarette. We were treated like lepers of biblical times, and this behavior continued for what seemed an eternity.

A few weeks later, however, Mr. Nix had a change of heart and lifted the moratorium, much to everyone's acclamation. The infamous four received an unconditional pardon, and things gradually settled back to normal. During the interim, though, I learned that smoking on the school campus was extremely dangerous in more ways than one, but it wasn't until later—the armadillo episode—that I finally took my last puff of a cigarette for a long, long time.

Our chief want in life is somebody who shall make us do what we can.

—Ralph Waldo Emerson

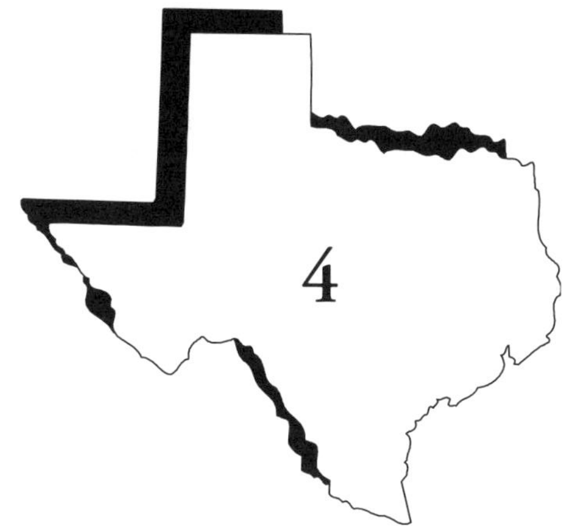

AHEAD OF MY TIME

FROM THE VERY BEGINNING, WATER REPRESENTED the most sought-after asset at the McKinley household. The previous owner of the house and forty acres, Joe Dickerson, had never seen fit to dig a well to supply drinking water for his family, and since he owned no cattle, there was no necessity for a pond either. Mother always talked about this oddity at great length and often used the curiosity to question Dad's decision to buy the farm in the first place.

"Why," she asked, "would anyone in their right mind, want to own land that yielded none of the life giving and sustaining elixir? That's makes no sense at all to me. Folks never settled on a piece of ground worth two cents, unless a creek, at the very least, ran through it. Why should we be any different? Yet here we are, landlocked so to speak. This place does not even have a well!"

Dad pledged to remedy the situation quickly, but he concentrated first on other priorities such as clearing areas for fields, where crops would be planted the following spring, and creating pastures, where cattle would forage when and if we ever got enough money to buy them. After that, additional cross fences, barns and the like had to be constructed. All this must have appeared a daunting challenge, but Dad threw himself into the undertaking with little fanfare.

I was not yet large enough to lend any worthwhile effort to the projects, so by necessity Mom became the first and lone assistant on which Dad relied to help him get the farm going. Of course, Mom's contribution outside the house came after she completed the cooking, washing dishes, doing the laundry, dusting, cleaning and scrubbing the floors—to mention only a few of her duties. Most of these household chores required water, the one thing that we had too little of. While she clearly understood Dad's chosen tasks to be important, Mom began to soon push the panic button, with good justification.

The farm's solitary store of water came from a cistern, located under one of the eaves of the house. Joe had constructed a gutter system of sorts that channeled rainwater from the roof into the collection point. This worked pretty well during the rainy seasons, but most summers about late July and August, the cistern either dried up completely, or the water became so low, wriggly-tails prevented us from using what remained. These were mosquito larvae found swimming on the surface of stagnant water.

With exhausted reserves, few options remained. Part of the time we placed a huge barrel on the horse- or mule-drawn wagon or into the truck and hauled what we could from the schoolhouse, which fortunately had a deep reservoir. During the driest months, however, much of the inventory came from the nearest creek. We boiled some for drinking and used the rest for bathing and other purposes.

Dad eventually tired of this predicament—helped along by Mom's continued pestering—so he decided to dig a well as close as possible to the back porch. Today the whole matter would have been much simpler. He could have called a driller who in short order would have located a suitable water quantity, and our problem would have been solved. Back then, however, our situation was far different. Due to limited financial resources—to the point of outright destitution—most wells in our community were hand-excavated. When I say by hand, I'm talking about backbreaking manual labor using posthole diggers, shovels and a simple crane system that helped hoist the loose dirt to the surface.

Before any work began, however, one had to know where to start. Since the entire process took so much time and toil, the initial location became all-important. For that my dad relied on a tried and true—although questionable—scientific approach known as water-witching. In other parts, they call it dowsing. By any name, though, some clarification is required. It seems that every rural community sported an old gentleman schooled in this art. I always thought that such mystics were related to Indian medicine men, who supposedly applied esoteric knowledge passed from one great shaman to the other.

Noble Garrett, Chinquapin's resident water-witcher, known throughout the county for his expertise, claimed that he could locate subterranean streams with the aid of a specialized device found throughout the ages. Noble's divining rod, however, was more novel than most. For some who may ridicule this notion, I'm telling you that I saw it with my own eyes.

The old man pulled from his overalls' back pocket a fresh willow branch, shaped similar to a chicken breastbone. He took the forked ends in his hands and started walking near our house. He explained that when the gadget sensed water, the small end would point toward the spot where my dad should dig. On that particular day Noble marched from one end of our property to the other with the willow stick standing straight and erect. It appeared that the venture held no promise whatsoever, and I had already concluded that this was nothing more than a bunch of malarkey, an old wives' tale based on superstition with its roots in some archaic discourse. Noble had almost given up himself but decided to give it one more try. He remarked that one possible location remained. Grandpa McKinley, who was with us that day, agreed.

Our house was built about five hundred feet below a red clay embankment that people called Hardy Hill. Its name became synonymous with hardship and untold struggles of man against nature, especially during rains when trucks and automobiles attempted to negotiate both sides of the steep slope without sliding into the ditches. The unfortunate many became stuck until rescued by friends, neighbors or good Samaritans.

Although Dad sympathized with their plight, he complained continually about the constant stream of wayfarers who found themselves bogged down to the axle or "up to the hind end of a good-sized turkey." Whether in daylight or darkness, irrespective of hour, they located our house, just a stone's throw away, knocked on the front door and requested assistance. More than once, Mom invited absolute strangers into our home to wait out the bad weather. A few of these short visits became all-nighters, when some storms lasted longer than usual. With the patience of Job, Mom put down blankets on the floor—making pallets, as we called them—and tried to make the unexpected guests as comfortable as could be expected. To my surprise, Mom never openly expressed exasperation. When I asked her how she held her temper in the face of such nonsense, she stated that it was the charitable thing to do. When the elements permitted, Dad muttered a little, trudged to the barn, harnessed the horse or mule and pulled the stranded vehicles from the clutches of the red quagmire. While some people left a couple of dollars for the family's effort, most just said, "Much obliged. I hope that we'll be able to return the favor sometime."

Trying times, you bet! But that is just the way it was. The main road crossed our property, and like it or not, drivers contended with the recurrent inconvenience, and all of us made the best of a bad situation.

My mother also lamented that, much to her embarrassment in her younger days, she and her siblings often pushed their dad's Model-T Ford up that same towering landmark, because the car's engine lacked both spark and power. She remarked that as a child she never imagined living so near Hardy Hill, yet ironically, years later, she dwelled in its shadow.

Noble and Grandpa McKinley, standing near the back of our house, looked toward the geological phenomenon in the distance and commented about the possibility of finding water atop it. In all my years (admitedly few), I had never heard such a ridiculous observation! Although I kept my opinion to myself, I couldn't understand how anything in liquid form could settle on an incline, yet not be found at its base. I had learned about that thing called gravity and I knew the common saying that *water always runs downhill.*

Dad agreed with my unspoken sentiments. Mom, however, voiced even greater apprehension and expressed complete disgust at the prospect of carrying pails about one-fifth of a mile, the distance walked after completing the round trip that would begin at our back door. But she finally accepted the concept that some water is better than none, no matter where it is, so the group fell in behind Noble, and the expedition continued.

When we arrived at the highest point, Noble became extremely excited. He yelled, "See, I told you so! Look at that willow stick!"

Sure enough, the apparatus twisted and turned in his hand so hard that I thought Noble's wrists would surely break under the stress. The stick pointed straight downward in a violent motion, identifying a spot where water would surely be discovered. After Noble and Grandpa left for home, the family remained at the summit and discussed the chore of digging the well. Mom still couldn't get over the extreme position, but as always she remarked that everything would work out eventually.

During the next few weeks Dad mustered all his energy, and armed with posthole diggers and a shovel, proceeded to grub through the red clay toward the precious commodity. We thought it great that the family would no longer have to rely on water hauled either from the school or Caney Creek. One enormous question remained: how far down would he have to go to find it? At about ten feet Dad grew a little agitated. At fifteen he began to question the wisdom of the great water witcher. At twenty feet he felt extremely lucky.

On that particular day, Mom brought lunch to the worksite. She spread the fixings of cold milk, water, biscuits, sausage and ham upon a cloth placed on the ground. She yelled for Dad to come up from the depths of the hole, take a well-deserved breather and eat at the same time.

Dad was always more than a little impatient. When he started something, he liked to finish it as quickly as possible, so he could move on to other projects of his choosing. Dad did not procrastinate and he was never satisfied unless he was busy doing one thing or another. When I was five I never quite understood this rationale. Work was something that I viewed with great suspicion. I felt that play was the most important thing in one's life and frankly, work got in the way of a good time.

Dad uttered a few obscenities under his breath as he climbed up the homemade ladder toward sunshine and the break that he viewed as more of a nuisance than anything. We washed our hands and had just sat down on the ground when a loud thud broke the silence. Stunned, we all looked toward the well. We arose and ran to the sound. After looking into the hole, our hearts raced. Saying nothing, we stared into the shaft, whose sides had literally given way and caved in. We could see only about ten feet; the rest of the hole was filled in completely with soil.

Then the reflections and what-ifs came. What if Mom had not fixed lunch at that exact time? What if Dad had reacted as usual and asserted that he would be finished in a few minutes, only to take an hour or more? What if he had been buried under ten feet of heavy red clay?

Of course, these were times before calling 911 and specialized rescue units. Besides, we had no telephone, and the nearest help was over two miles away. The answer finally came with a bleak awareness. Our small family just stood there in a state of shock, thinking about how we had just avoided disaster and how fortunate we were.

Dad, still stunned by his near-death experience, remarked, "I suppose that it just wasn't my time."

CHINQUA WHERE?

That was one of the first instances that I recognized a near miss, a life-threatening scenario. I had never been exposed to the potential loss of a loved one, and from that time, life became a lot more special.

As Mom had so stoically remarked that everything would work out, so it did. Dad seemed to forget about the accident quickly and resumed the difficult undertaking, although steadily grumbling about having to remove the soil and gravel for a second time. He said something about hating to plough the same furrow twice in a row. I failed to get the message, but it didn't matter. I rarely understood such aphorisms. This time, however, Dad took precautions and installed casings as he went to prevent a repetition of the recent calamity.

At about thirty feet, he finally hit pay dirt! Mom kept saying that this was good water, in that it held no discernible impurities. I was not yet properly educated in such things as iron, sulfur or other chemical contents. Unfortunately Dad used different lining materials for the last ten feet of the project. The boards taken from a recently felled red oak tree quickly gave the water a much different and less appealing taste. Mom blamed Dad for ruining the quality, but even so, it represented a vast improvement over what we had in the past.

From that point forward, the completed well contributed greatly to our daily existence, and in the process, created some of my unforgettable memories. Since our house contained no plumbing of any type, taking inside baths required quite an effort. We placed Mom's Number 2 galvanized washtub in the middle of the living room. Then we made repeated trips up the hill, drew water and carried it, bucket by agonizing bucket down to the house where we emptied the contents into a large pan and heated it on the butane stove. After that, we filled the tub to about one-half of its capacity.

There was, of course, a good reason for the restriction. If you've ever carried water by hand, at *any* distance, you will call to mind how the grip digs into your fingers and gnaws at the palms of your hands. In trying to limit the agony, we reached a fitting compromise and settled on half a tub rather than a full one. At times, we expressed the opinion that, after all the work involved, we were just too tired to bathe. Nevertheless, we took our respective turns in the common tub. Being the youngest, I always went first, then Dad and finally Mom, who described this family ritual as a lesson in conservation. She remarked that we had to save all we could, and that she always tried to follow the advice detailed in the old expression: Waste not, want not.

Talk about labor intensive! That's all I thought about when I heard Mom declare that bath time was at hand.

CHINQUA WHERE?

Given the aspects of daily life, the well probably made more of an impression on me than most of the other features found on our property. It not only served as a source for drinking and bathing, it also supplied the water that Mom used for washing purposes. A few feet from its base, Dad built a stand under the shade of a gnarled blackjack tree. The Number 2 tub and a scrub board completed the elementary workstation ensemble. He also strung a clothesline, a strand of wire stretched between two trees, to hold the wet clothes until dried by the breezes supplied by good old Mother Nature. Nearby Mom kept two huge blackened pots that she used for making lye soap and doing the laundry. This staging area held many a ferocious clash between woman and dirty outfits, along with numerous other weekly revelries, one in particular.

On washday, my job was to supply the wood. Mom drew one bucket of water after the other and poured it into both pots until each reached the precise level. Then she lit the fire—and the boiling began! She used one cauldron for washing and the other for rinsing, the latter we lovingly called "ranching."

No, I have not erroneously referred to ranching, as in the raising of cattle or horses, and I certainly know the difference between that and rinsing clothes. I have merely used the spelling variation to illustrate a point of interest. Comedians and most of our adopted cousins above the

Mason-Dixon Line have long poked fun and commented about how native Texans often mispronounce various words, leading to total confusion and complete frustration. Throughout my adulthood, I've had a great deal of fun with two specific examples. One must exercise the utmost care when conversing with a good old boy or girl from the Lone Star State.

When you talk about *all,* you could be referring to *oil,* the black gold that lubricates moving parts; *all,* the entire group of folks or one half of y'all; or *All,* the name brand dishwashing detergent. The same dialectic applies to *ranch,* as in *ranch,* the accumulated acreage of some landowner; *wrench,* a tool used to loosen a nut on a bolt; *wrench,* the twisting and injuring of an individual's back when picking up too heavy an object; or *rinse,* as in to rinse the soap suds from one's garments. So it is incumbent on the person inquiring about such declarations to be very explicit! Believe me, if you don't, you will never know which end is up, and you will wind up tied in knots.

One summer my mom began a tradition that continued for at least a year or two. After finishing the weekly washing chore and the rinse water had cooled somewhat, she ordered me to bathe. I was a little apprehensive at first, believing that the hot water might scald the hair from my hide as it did when we butchered and cleaned hogs. But Mom tested the temperature and said that it was just right. So I looked around to make sure that no one peeked, threw off my clothes, double-checked the temperature with a big toe and crawled right in. *Not bad*, I thought.

Mom always took every opportunity to rid me of those terrible smells received from outdoor play with the family dogs and cats. So there I was at age five and six, naked as a jaybird, splashing around in an iron kettle stationed at the peak of Hardy Hill, not more than sixty feet from the main road. Somehow I didn't seem to mind a bit. Besides, there was not much traffic on Farm to Market 1751, and my skinny body remained shielded from view as long as I stayed beneath the rim.

For some reason, however, no one ever planned properly for what followed after my special soak. Believe it or not, we could never remember to bring along a fresh towel or a change of clothes, so I sped, totally exposed, for the five hundred feet or so and into our house to get dressed. This affair, however unusual, gradually evolved into custom.

Great exhilaration followed every successful run. But I sought at every turn to improve my technique, so I pushed the boundaries! I developed a knack for arriving at the back door just in time to avoid being seen by passing motorists. Stealth became my strongest point, and for months on end, my perfect record stood in spite of several close scares. But as the sportscasters say, a win is a win regardless of the score, and the impressive string only added to my feeling of invincibility. But one afternoon, I fell from the ranks of the undefeated when faced with a surprise attack just about the halfway mark of my normal trek. A black Ford, traveling the road that lay parallel to my track-and-field course, came out of nowhere.

I remember the feeling as if it happened yesterday. The car slowed to a crawl, and the man who drove pointed me out to a lady passenger. Both seemed to get a big kick out of the situation, but I was more than a little humiliated. Afterward I announced to Mom that I would never do that again, and I didn't.

During the 1970s, country singer Ray Stevens released a popular hit song entitled "The Streak." I also recall that someone, clad only in his birthday attire, ran across the stage at an Academy Awards presentation in front of a national television audience. Talk about exposure! But regardless of one's views about such behavior, an entire subculture developed around this manner of exhibition-ism. I always considered that the folks who followed suit with this startling recreation had nothing on me, because prior to 1951, as a resident of Chinquapin, Texas, I may have invented this diversion when on countless occasions, I streaked down Hardy Hill to our house in the valley be-low.

THEY CALL ME "THE STREAK!"

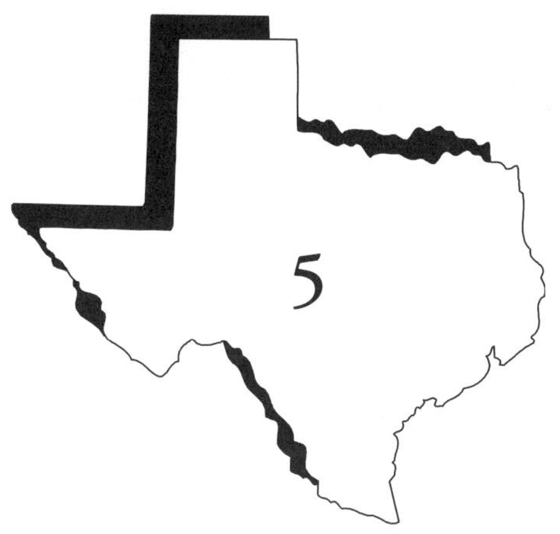

5

FIRST DAY OF SCHOOL

A S SOME OF YOU MAY REMEMBER, THE FIRST DAY of school was both an exciting and terrifying experience. For me, however, the event carries additional merit in that I learned a valuable lesson early on—to neither accept nor react to suggestions from my fellow classmates, at least until I took the time to reason and study the consequences a little more thoroughly.

On that hot September day in 1949, I was the typical bright-eyed kid, dressed in striped overalls and a new starched shirt made from a designer flour sack. Back in those days and even earlier I'm sure, the folks who manufactured cattle feed and flour implemented a new and fantastic marketing paradigm. They discovered that housewives would purchase their particular line of products—and remain loyal afterwards—if the contents were packaged inside sacks sewn with material, both in texture and design that could be suitably adapted to making dresses, shirts and such. Don't be surprised now; skilled advertisers have always been around to help you part with your hard-earned cash.

Pure economics prompted most wives in the rural environment to become very selective when they went to town to buy goods. I remember that my own mom took considerable time and care hand-picking special sacks due to their particular colors and patterns. She used the fabric to fashion shirts for me and dresses for her.

After finishing my garments, Mom must have relied on more than the required amount of starch during the ironing process, because when I wore them for the first time, the shirts almost rubbed the skin from both my neck and arms. Anyway, the new apparel made quite an impression on my teachers, who offered rave reviews. I never knew whether mine represented the best-looking examples on campus, or perhaps Mom was the only one who took the time to use an iron and set those distinctive creases before sending her kid off to school. Who really knows? Regardless of the explanation, I really enjoyed all the glowing compliments.

I had always been extremely shy, a characteristic that I attribute to being an only child in a rustic setting with few close neighbors. As such, I learned quickly to entertain myself at home, running and playing like a wild maniac with my trusted pal, a hound named Lep, and a stick horse usually made from a discarded mop handle, which I called by various names depending on the genre of the daily playtime fantasy. Thunder Cloud, War Bonnet, Trigger and Silver represented a few of the many.

Mother was a former teacher with more than eight years of experience behind her, so the training for my earliest venture into academia took on special significance. In truth, however, she was much more involved in the process than I would have liked. But as a proud member of the Veterans of Teaching Wars, she always instructed me to get along with others, to be quiet when the situation dictated, and above the rest, to respect and extend courtesy to elders, especially schoolteachers. Somewhere in those philosophical back roads, a six-year-old can become somewhat confused when presented with too many options, and as a result, take a wrong turn into a path where predestined ambush awaits.

The Buddy Burns and Joe Dickerson families were some of our neighbors who lived up the dirt road about five miles. There were several boys in those households, and I recall one in particular, Marvin Dickerson, the older brother of Jo-Boy, Mabel Lois and Mary Lou, individuals whom I had known all my life. Marvin, though young in years, had already claimed the justly awarded title of chief instigator of mischief in the community, and he sought every opportunity to defend and demonstrate his proficiency in front of any audience that provided the best forum.

As the bus stopped at our house on my first day of school, I timidly got on and took a seat way in the back, hoping and praying that no one would speak to me. I told you I was bashful! As the driver made his usual rounds, several of the kids failed to get on. Their parents held them out for the time being, sending word that they would not be allowed to attend class until the crops were in, usually around the first of October. That seemed curious to me, but later I learned that even then, many youngsters, regardless of age, were expected to contribute to the farm's success, despite school-attendance mandates. They were an integral part of the labor pool on which parents depended. For some, work came first; formal education, second.

When the bus pulled in front of the schoolhouse, I exited and proceeded to the center of the playground, already abuzz with various types of activity. I stood there briefly, looking forlorn and without any purpose. In preparation for the beginning of the school term, Dad had given me one of the closest haircuts ever, with as much ear showing as possible. I was more than a little self-conscious about my appearance. He used manually operated hand-held clippers—which I still own today—all the while demanding that I quit squirming around. The being still part was a hard thing to do, because those antiquated tools lived up to a well-earned reputation for pulling the hair of anyone who dared sit in my dad's barber chair. Cousins Wayne and Jerry Wright should well remember their respective close shaves with those same old shears.

Anyhow, when I got to the middle of the schoolyard, I heard, "Hey, little boy, come over here."

When I turned toward the voice, I recognized the guys who were calling, some of the Burnses and Marvin Dickerson. The latter remarked that he wanted me to do something.

I answered promptly, "Sure. What?"

Now that must have been one of the dumbest replies that I ever phrased, at least until then.

"Do you see that little dumb-ass standing over there?" Marvin asked, pointing to a fellow student about my size and stature.

"Yep," I responded. What about him?"

"Well," he asked, "do you know him?"

"No. Why?"

"Okay," he said. "Now here's what you should do...."

Since I had never seen this boy before, he must have been an outsider. Marvin explained further that in order for me to become one of the guys, I needed to show them how tough I was. To demonstrate that fully, I had to double my fist and hit this kid in the stomach as hard as I could, the harder, the better. Preferably still, if I could knock the breath out of him, this would be the true test that I would surely pass with flying colors.

Admittedly this seemed quite odd! I had never been in a fistfight before, but all this school business was new to me, it being the first day and all.

With the benefit of hindsight, I should have suspected that something was up when Marvin couldn't stop laughing amid the delivery of such serious and important instructions. The Burns boys seemed to be really enjoying themselves as well, and I couldn't help but wonder what was so funny. Believing that the fellows would certainly bust a gut before they let me in on the private joke, I had just about decided to walk away—but something kept running through my mind concerning what Mom taught me, that I should always respect my elders. I realize now that this sounds unbelievable, but at that moment, the whole thing appeared perfectly logical.

So, I told Marvin that I would do the best that I could. I doubled my fist, walked toward the boy, tapped his shoulder from the back, and when he turned around, I let him have it with all the strength that a six-year-old could muster. His face went expressionless, and he doubled over in pain and anguish.

I concluded that I must have succeeded at the dutiful task when I looked at Marvin and the Burns boys and saw their delight—but something was wrong. The boy couldn't catch his breath, so I began to worry that he might be permanently injured. After a few moments, however, he gained the ability not only to breathe, but also to scream in terrifying tones loud enough to wake the dead.

A stream of tears accompanied a screech that sounded something like, "Why did you hit me?" Then came the expected, "Boy, are you going to be in trouble!"

As the melee continued, I felt that surely I must have gained acceptance into the fraternity of manhood. The boy, still crying and screaming at the top of his voice, ran from the playground and into the front door of the school building.

One by one, Marvin and the other guys stepped forward and offered hearty congratulations. Smiles, pats on the back and glorious praises filled the air. My spirits rose to the level of achieved knighthood, but the glory was short-lived. Only seconds later, it seemed, I witnessed a horrible spectacle that few should expect to see in their lifetimes. Everyone stepped back, and I stood alone in a circle that measured approximately twenty feet across. I wondered, *What the heck is going on?* Then I turned and saw the boy, whose plow I had just cleaned, walk in my direction. Actually, a fast trot is a better description.

To his side and holding his hand came a lady who looked somewhat familiar. She kept asking him, "Where is that fellow who just hit you?"

Silence fell on the playground, and you could have heard a pin drop. All eyes clicked toward me as the boy pointed my way and yelled, "That's him! There he is! He's the one, Mama!"

That last word, *Mama*, got my undivided attention. Something was just not right.

I had seen this woman before, and in fact, Mom and I talked to her once while in San Augustine. She was alone on that particular occasion, and I didn't know or care whether she had any kids of her own. But today would be much different, because I would find out there were two children in her family. In fact, I had just met the younger one during the hands-on introduction to Stephen, son of Pauline Collins, my first-grade teacher!

Mrs. Collins promptly grabbed me by the nape of the neck and shouted like a drill sergeant, ordering me to go along with her to the classroom. As I was being dragged along, my heart pounded louder than ever before. I thought that cardiac arrest would surely follow. My eyes blurred, my knees weakened, and my legs shook. I was too scared to talk. Tears were almost at the point of

HE'S THE ONE MAMA!

explosion, and I came pretty darn close to wetting my overalls.

One kid yelled in the background, "Mrs. Collins is going to whip you plumb half to death," while another shouted, "Betcha gonna get your nose in the ring!"

Clearly, these observations caused a lot of consternation and outright hysteria. I could relate to the whipping issue, but as for this nose and ring thing, I had serious queries. My brain started working overtime probing for clues. Although my individual pool of experience lacked depth, I had seen Dad on numerous occasions place rings in hogs' noses. He explained why, but I soon forgot about it, figuring that I had better things to occupy my mind. Now I wished that I had paid more attention. *It has nothing to do with punishment*, I thought. Still, I doubted that a teacher would resort to such cruel behavior against one of her students—but I couldn't be sure.

When Mrs. Collins and I arrived at her office, which was nothing more than a desk in the middle of that great hall called a classroom, she advised me to sit and think about what I had just done. In a little bit, she asked, "Why?"

As I searched in vain for the most suitable answer, she explained that hitting her son was no different from slugging some other kid, but somehow I really didn't accept that conclusion, nor do I to this day. I tried to ignore the question—hoping that it would just go away, but Mrs. Collins repeated it, only this time she meant business.

Finally I broke! *There's no use of holding back now, I thought. I'm not going down alone.* I had heard actors repeat those two lines in gangster movies, and I believed that each represented pretty sound advice, given the tight spot and the urgency of the setting.

Like the torrent of water rushing over Niagara Falls, I described the mishap, from beginning to unfortunate ending, and even named Marvin and the others as participants in the conspiracy. Participants, heck! I blamed them for the whole shebang. The teacher bit her lower lip and said nothing.

Mom's steady inventory of recitations always included the one about telling the truth will set you free. Maybe, Mrs. Collins had never heard that. Since she still appeared madder than a wet hen, I feared that the granddaddy of all punishments loomed just around the corner. I suspected that in due course, she would reach into one of her desk drawers and pull out some horrendous paddle, the kind with holes bored in the wood for maximum effect. Long before, I had heard a lot about those devices of persecution. But for the sake of me, I could never remember a time when anyone spoke of that new phraseology nose and ring.

The wait seemed interminable, but when she eventually spoke, Mrs. Collins revealed the mettle from whence great teachers are made. To my astonishment and complete amazement, she calmly began the discussion. With poise extraordinaire, she explained that even though tendencies of violence would not be tolerated in her class, she was not going to use the issue as justification to heat up my tail end. After all, this was the first day of class, and everyone deserves a second chance.

Wise teacher, I thought. *My opinion exactly.*

Feeling somewhat better about my chances, I had to ask, "What about the ring in the nose?"

She cracked a smile and then bent over in laughter. Mrs. Collins walked to the blackboard, took a piece of chalk, and asked me to step forward. I was sure then I should have kept my mouth shut.

The teacher said that she was going to show me something. She directed me to stand as near the board as possible, on my tiptoes, then press my nose against the surface. When I did, she took the chalk and drew a ring around the area where the small imprint remained. Then she explained that when students became too unruly, they had to stand at attention with their *nose in the ring*, not with a *ring in their nose*.

One can only imagine my reaction when I at last understood. Mrs. Collins' succinct description provided me with an immediate sense of comfort, and as bizarre as it may seem, both teacher and student gained from the exchange. I must have given Mrs. Collins some dimension of comic relief that morning, because she now seemed to be in a very good mood. She told me to return to the playground, because school was about to take up shortly.

But as I strode toward the door, I had not the vaguest idea about the teacher's expertise in handling discipline problems, nor did I yet understand that she exercised a touch of psychological discretion in the process. I believed that without saying it in so many terms, she felt sorry for me and let the crisis pass because of my complete ignorance and pitiful-looking mannerisms. As a rank amateur, I must have been some sorry sight, standing there all red-eyed and shaky, clad in those striped overalls with the starched homemade shirt, questioning whether I would be the first kid in Chinquapin history to wear nose jewelry.

I eventually learned a lot from that encounter, things like compassion, forgiveness, respect for teachers, word placement, peer pressure, but most of all, never, under any circumstances, should one belt the teacher's son on the first day of school! Maybe the second is a better choice? I'm just kidding!

Later that year when Mrs. Collins caught me dipping Dora Wagstaff's pigtails in a bottle of ink, I had occasion to stand at the front of the class with my nose in the ring. Although extremely embarrassed, I weathered this form of ridicule with the greatest of ease. Besides, it beat the alternative.

Given that males now wear earrings on a pretty regular basis, a friend asked me recently whether I had ever thought seriously about joining the craze.

"Whatever turns your crank," I responded, "but it isn't my style."

When he tried to change the topic, I quickly seized the opportunity to set up a joke and have a few laughs. I added, "But I did put my nose in the ring more than a few times!"

Much to my solemn regret, this statement never evoked a single response.

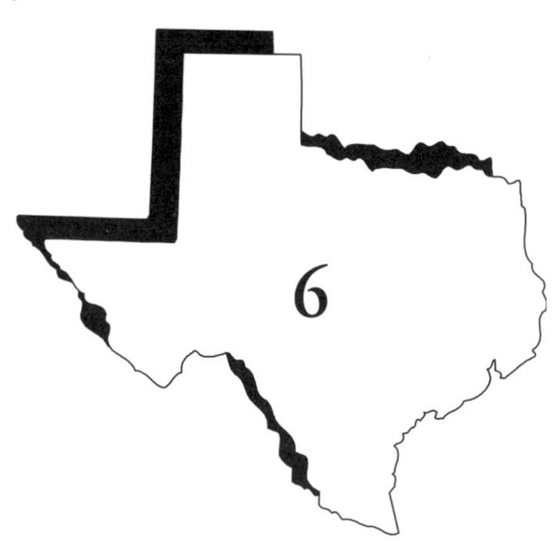

COLD BISCUITS AND TERROR

URING THE FALL OF 1949, DAD NEGOTIATED A deal with my granddad Wright to tear down an aged barn in exchange for the used lumber, tin and other materials. When Dad divulged his intention to me, I asked if he could use a good hand, and as usual, he said that it was okay with him as long as Mom approved. After several hours of plain old-fashioned begging, I finally sold Mom on the idea that I should tag along and lend whatever assistance I could. So one Saturday morning we set out for the old place, the term affectionately used by all family members to describe the dilapidated house and the surrounding hundred and sixty-something acres.

I viewed the old place as really special. My mom, her sisters and brothers were born and raised there, and it is where my grandmother Exa Wright and her infant daughter died. The land on which the home stood had been previously owned by my great-grandfather, Jesse Miles Drawhorn, who for some mysterious reason sold it to Daddy Wright, then left for parts unknown.

Not much, however, remained by 1949. Remnants of a formerly productive peach orchard stood in disrepair, and the red farmland that had supported a family and yielded cash crops of cotton, corn and peanuts lay fallow. Small trees and underbrush covered the rolling meadows, where cattle previously thrived. As for the dwelling itself, it crumbled at all points and seemed to gasp while struggling for a last breath. No vestige of furnishings could be found within the four decrepit main rooms, with one exception: a homemade gun rack, nailed above the inside front door facing, stood as mute testimony of a time when my granddad used to store his 12-gauge shotgun there. Wallpaper, which in the past had so brightly colored the interior, fell by the chunks onto the uneven and rotted wooden floors. Pillagers, looters and other local marauders had taken most everything else, leaving behind only shattered window panes and a few shredded cloth curtains that hung in disarray. Other once-proud structures, including the detached garage and smokehouse, leaned and appeared as though they too would fall at any moment.

But all was not total doom and gloom. Irrespective of the property's despondent facade, bountiful treasures that charmed and magnetized a six-year-old could be seen everywhere. Even with its once shiny surface deeply scratched and faded, the old organ survived somehow on the home's back porch. Although the musical apparatus no longer operated, I banged on the keys and imagined how beautiful it might have sounded during years gone by. I had always questioned the existence of that particular instrument in the Wright household in the first place, as my grandfather had been expelled from one house of worship because he opposed the use of a piano. This issue has always been a paradox to me, but I suppose that one has to look carefully for distinct differences between an organ and a piano, and whether it is played at home or in church.

The most favorite relic, however, was the rusted chassis of a Model A Ford that someone parked in the back under a large oak tree and simply left for the ravages of time. For years, I remember sitting at its wheel, making sputtering noises like an engine, and traveling to faraway places. I suspected that I could have lived within the confines of that beloved artifact, and because I played in it infrequently, I hated to leave for home.

Once I offered a proposition to Daddy Wright for me to secure the antique Ford. As he was a shrewd tradesman, I knew that I had to make it sound like he would lose nothing of value in the transaction. My convincing argument began, "If you give me the old piece of junk (it hurt me deeply to call it that name) I will gladly take it off your hands and have my dad move it to our house."

He agreed without a whimper, but that was the easy part! The real problem came when I approached Dad to take on the work of moving it. Finally, after a long-drawn-out and serious debate that took place over several days, I convinced him to see it my way. During the following week, we spent several hours using a do-it-your-self crane system, attempting to hoist the bulky skeleton of a car unto a one-horse wagon. Dad wanted no assistance from the neighbors—he was just that way—so Mom and I pitched in. But no matter how hard we tried, we never successfully lifted the body high enough to accomplish our task. Eventually, with dusk drawing near, we abandoned the undertaking altogether, and even though Dad issued numerous apologies, nothing helped me get over the feeling that I had deserted a cherished friend.

I also explored the collapsing barns that yet contained a few well-worn ploughs and harnesses. I wandered through these abandoned buildings and my imagination ran wild. If presented today, I swear that I would

WHERE'S MY SELECTION?

and I crossed the road in front of our house and took the shortcut through the woods. As the crow flies, the old place lay about a mile and a half away. When possible, I skipped along. But when the woods became too thick, I dodged briars and thorn bushes and tried to keep low-hanging tree limbs from slapping me in the face. Dad was on the constant lookout for squirrels; in fact he'd brought along his shotgun just in case one appeared at the right time. Country folks always had to consider where the next meal was coming from.

Before long we found ourselves at the banks of Chinquapin Creek, where we stopped to get a cool drink of water and rest for a bit. After a few minutes Dad became impatient, so we continued our trip. We arrived at the clearing in front of the house by about 8 a.m. and soon we were busy dismantling the barn.

Dad assigned me the duty of pulling nails out of the boards and straightening them for reuse. At the time, I could see no rational explanation for such pointless actions, but we were practicing recycling, that recent ecological phenomenon. The real reason lay in the fact that we had no money to purchase new nails or lumber, and Dad needed the materials to build a much needed barn at our place.

Issuing stern warnings about my responsibility, Dad said that he intended this as a day of work. Play, he cautioned, would have to wait for other times. That directive hit hard, especially since I could see that Ford chassis sitting under the tree not more than fifty feet away. But work I did! Resisting the temptation to gaze in the direction of the auto, I spent the entire morning pulling and straightening at least a dozen nails, which I might add were the old-fashioned square ones. Admittedly, I was more fascinated by the shape of those nails than with my individual production.

Dad admonished me several times and added, "Boy, if you continue at that snail's pace, we'll be here till spring."

About noon, Dad stopped, wiped the sweat from his face, walked toward the oak tree and my car, sat down and peered into the paper sack that contained—you know what! He pulled out a biscuit, opened it with his knife, inserted one of those cold sausages and proceeded to eat. He offered one to me. With a pitiful look of rejection, I politely refused. Several minutes passed without conversation.

Dad had just bit into his second biscuit when I asked, "What else do you have in that sack?"

Opening it again, he looked inside and responded, "I don't see anything in there but a couple of biscuits and sausages." He asked whether I had changed my mind and wanted some. I said that I had not.

"I don't like cold biscuits and sausages," I mumbled. Sitting with wounded pride, I couldn't understand why Mom had sent her boy off to do man's work without packing something good to eat.

This is inhumane, I thought, *and as soon as we get home this afternoon, I plan to really talk to her about this injustice.*

In about thirty minutes, Dad resumed work, and he recommended that I do likewise. If you thought that my morning's production of nail pulling was less than satisfactory, you should have seen it by mid-afternoon. Why I even considered a work stoppage of sorts, but I knew that Dad would regard that action as outright rebellion. And as with czars and other despots, he would probably dispel such ideas of newly found independence with swift and harsh retribution. So I carried on with my paltry exercise and attempted to look a lot busier than I actually was.

By 2 p.m., though, I couldn't ignore my hunger pains. Somewhere during his lunch, I lost count of the number of biscuits and sausages that Dad had eaten. When the twinges became almost unbearable, my thoughts drifted toward that paper sack still lying under the tree, and I wondered whether anything remained of its original contents. But I caught myself and reestablished some degree of reasonability. By 3 p.m., however, I was so hungry that those cold biscuits and sausage began to generate a certain allure from which I could not escape.

Perhaps, I speculated, *this is the proper time to try something new. After all, a man has to expand his horizons.* I summoned all my strength, took a deep breath and asked Dad about any possible leftovers.

He grinned and kidded me a little by saying, "I didn't think that you cared for cold biscuits and sausage, son."

That's what I call rubbing salt in an open wound. Dad continued, "But just in case you've changed your mind, I left a couple in there for you."

That's what I wanted to hear! I walked over to the tree and opened the sack, still praying for an outside chance that Mom might have placed some other goodies in there for me, but no such luck! Two cold biscuits and sausages stared back at me. I had gone too far to turn back now, and for the first time in my life, I began to understand what the phrase eating crow meant.

Following Dad's example, I opened a biscuit with my trusted Barlow knife, inserted the sausage, held my breath, closed my eyes and took a bite. Much to my surprise, this was not a bad meal. *That tastes pretty good,* I thought. *In fact, it's downright delicious!*

It didn't take long for me to devour those few remaining morsels and soon I was back at work pulling and straightening nails. Dad said nothing, but from the corner of my eye, I saw him grinning from ear to ear.

Around 4 p.m., we stopped for the day. Clouds were rolling in, and it looked a lot like rain. Dad mentioned that he would complete the job on the following Monday. We needed to get back and feed the livestock. Even though I was tired and dreaded the long walk home, I felt a little different, and in some unusual aspect, I was extremely proud of the way that I handled the afternoon meal situation.

Our return took a little different route and the trip itself remained pretty much uneventful, until we came to an edge of a clearing in the underbrush. In the misty background, I saw the faint figure of a rustic, unpainted house, which resembled that of my granddad Wright. My dad always loved practical jokes, and briefly, I thought that he played a trick on me by merely circling in the woods. Perhaps we were right back where we started.

As I asked him about it, he looked at me and said, "Be quiet boy! This is the old Marion Henley place."

I had no idea who or what he was talking about, but Dad had a sense of firmness in his voice. He issued caustic instructions for me to stand still in my tracks and make no noise while he crept in for a closer look. I couldn't quite get a handle on what was happening. But I did as I was told, and before long Dad stepped quietly into the clearing.

Watching his every movement, I said aloud, "Dad must have a lot of Indian blood in him, because he walks through the woods and underbrush just like a brave stalking a deer."

When I blinked, he disappeared. I remained there for what seemed hours, gazing at the house and noting each minute detail. The shutters were loose and tattered, while the collapsed wooden shingles on the roof exposed rafters underneath. The wind blew through the missing windows, and occasionally it seemed that the house even groaned.

"That is a ghastly sight," I muttered. "This is no place to be."

Besides, the tall pines swaying in the breeze gave me a weird feeling. It would be dark soon, and I didn't relish being out in these woods with Heaven knows what? My breathing became heavier, and my heart pounded. Dad was nowhere to be seen.

"Where is he?" I questioned with rising anxiety. "Why would he leave me alone out here in this God-forsaken place?"

Finally, I saw him walk out of the front door, look back and almost run down the fragmented steps toward my direction. I could hardly wait for him to get back to where

I stood, and when he did, I filled the air with questions. He said, "Be quiet son! We need to get out of here fast! I'll tell you about it later."

When we crossed Chinquapin Creek, he remarked that he thought it would be safe to stop for a while. "Safe from what?" I asked in a trembling voice.

Dad ordered me to sit on the ground, and he would tell the story. Even in broad daylight, my thoughts raced and my eyes brightened. I could hardly believe what he told me that fall afternoon. It seems that Marion Henley had lived in this area long ago. The badly deteriorated house and surrounding acreage had been one of the better farms around, but years of neglect had taken their toll. After the old man died, none of his family members wanted to live that far back in the pine thicket, so the house lay vacant. (That's when I realized there were no roads leading to the house place.) It seems that some vagrants occupied the house during the Great Depression, and a fight over a bottle of rotgut whiskey resulted in the death of one of those unfortunate souls. According to Dad's recollections, the victim's spirit remained, and sometimes it took the form of a hideous monster that everyone called Bloody Bones.

I asked, "What does he look like?"

Dad responded, "Nobody really knows for sure. If you see Bloody Bones, you're done for! He never leaves anyone alive to tell. I forgot about this tale briefly, but luckily for us, I remembered before it was too late. That's why I almost broke my neck getting out of the house. Let's go! We need to hurry and get home before dark, because that's when Bloody Bones does his dastardly deeds."

I couldn't let on that I was scared stiff. I wanted to act every bit the part of a grownup, but I was never so glad to see our house as I was that late afternoon. I reveled in the comfort and security of my own room.

Several days later, Uncle Arnold came to visit. Since we had only two bedrooms, Uncle "Mutt," as I called him, slept in mine. He loved to tell ghost stories and I loved to hear them. Unfortunately one night after we had retired, I asked Mutt if he had ever heard anyone mention Bloody Bones.

He replied, "As a matter of fact I have. Do you want me to tell you about my experiences with the old rogue?"

I pulled the cover to my eyes, and answered, much to my regret, "Sure."

It's been so long now that I can't recall much about his yarns, other than the effects afterward when I screamed and ran to my parents' room where I jumped into their bed in stark terror. But after a while, I gathered enough strength to reenter my bedroom where Mutt lay awake, smiling. Each time, I begged for additional details, followed with a promise not to flee in the usual style.

No matter how hard I tried, however, each time resulted in shameful retreat. These escapades continued for several nights and even repeated themselves for a few years, until I finally decided that Bloody Bones was nothing more than a figment of somebody's wild creativity.

Once Dad was working on some pipeline out of state, which he did about six months of each year. During those absences, Mom and I usually stayed nights with my grandparents because she was afraid of the dark. When we returned home from one of those nightly visits, Mom checked our mailbox. She reached in, pulled out a single item, looked a little puzzled and handed it to me. Stunned a little, I held a horror comic book in my hands. Wide-eyed, I asked, "Where did this come from?"

She replied that she had no clue. There was no postage, no return address and no evidence that it had ever been mailed. To this day, we never learned how that parcel made its way into our mail receptacle. I do know, however, that I read and reread that book and experienced continuous nightmares about the stories. I can describe the contents still, even after all those years.

I have no first-hand proof that ghosts, poltergeists and spirits exist, although I cannot deny that such notions have always intrigued me. But way back then, I concluded that maybe—just maybe, Bloody Bones had visited our house the previous night. Perhaps, under the cover of darkness, he left that little present in the form of a horror comic book just to remind me that he was still there, lurking and waiting for the right moment to claim another victim.

Then, as now, I find that the combination of dusk, a cloudy night and the rustling of trees in a gentle wind leave me with an unsettled feeling. You may find this quite amusing, but no one, including you, is quiet sure what happens way back in those East Texas piney woods when the darkness comes, the owls screech and the trees wail in the breeze.

Wisdom is ofttimes nearer when we stoop than when we soar.

—William Wordsworth

A BUDDING SALESMAN

AS INDICATED EARLIER, I WAS EXTREMELY SHY AS a youngster, especially around strangers. However, when dealing with people I knew while growing up, problems with communication never surfaced.

One day I perused through our current issue of *Progressive Farmer,* and in the back I spotted an advertisement that caught my fancy. The ad pointed out that students could earn fabulous prizes by selling a tried-and-true product door to door. Since this seemed a perfectly good idea at the time, I read further and began to daydream about those fantastic prizes. What about that wristwatch, the radio, or better still, the bow and arrow set? By selling White Cloverine Salve, one could really make a haul.

The more that I studied about it, the more excited I became about that bow and arrow. I needed a new set anyway. Most country boys depended on slingshots or guns. I had a bow and arrow. Not that I ever killed or even wounded anything with it, but there was something special about taking a homemade bow, shooting an arrow at some target, and then looking for what seemed an eternity to find it lying in the grass or amongst a bunch of weeds and bushes. After I finally found the arrow, the whole process was repeated over and again.

Somehow I expected that a professionally manufactured set would improve my hunting skills, and armed with that new weaponry, surely I would be able to bring home squirrels for my mom to prepare for cooking. I had to find a way to earn that particular prize. That's all I thought about for days on end. I spoke to Mom about it. She issued cautious advice and asked the great question: To whom did I expect to sell all that salve?

"With all the known cures that White Cloverine Salve is famous for," I responded, "why, everyone we know will want to buy some."

The population of Chinquapin was small, but to me at such a young age, I exaggerated the numbers by quite a bit. Regardless, with the plan formulated, I approached Dad with my marketing idea. He offered no real resistance, so I completed the order form and mailed it.

Sure enough, a few days later a package arrived. The cylindrical container held two dozen cans of the product on which my sales career would soon be founded. While opening the package, I could hardly wait to get out there, sell my stock, and then receive my new bow and arrow.

I convinced myself there was nothing to it! All I'd have to do is visit my aunt, uncle and grandparents, Sam Dickerson, his parents, Ray Dickerson, and few other neighbors. There's no way that they could resist purchasing a product that remedies a person's chapped hands, chapped face, chapped lips, sunburn, windburn, minor cuts and burns, rashes and other skin irritations, along with a myriad of other maladies too numerous to list.

I well remember the exuberant feeling as I left the house bright and early the next morning to make my first sales pitch. About a mile down the road, I approached Aunt Johnnie B. Wright, who promptly stated that she didn't need any of that old stuff. Lonnie and Gladys Dickerson didn't need any either, but at the next stop, Grandpa McKinley purchased one can. My attitude perked up immediately, and I temporarily forgot about the earlier setbacks. I had finally made my first sale, and now only twenty-three cans remained.

Ray Dickerson and Annie didn't participate in the chance of a lifetime, and that was a shocker. At first I felt a little perturbed that Lee Allen's parents turned me away, but I recalled the time that Mom dragged me to their house to buy some fresh purple-hull peas and some of those big, tasty, vine-ripe tomatoes. Earlier that morning, I had a severe headache, and I did not want to go traipsing all over creation. I told Mom that I wanted to stay at home and nurse my pain. She would not hear of it, however, so I went along, griping to high heavens.

After we returned home, Mom cooked up a mess of peas, as we called the dish, and served them during a late lunch. I chopped up a couple of the tomatoes and placed them inside a bowl, filled with peas and pot liquor (the liquid left after boiling whatever it is that one is cooking). That's the first time I ever tried that exceptional combination, which turned out to be one of my most favorite meals. Anyway, the headache soon subsided, and I determined that the definitive treatment for that nuisance lay in the form of eating peas and tomatoes.

Remembering that particular affair, I soon issued a reprieve to Ray and Annie, after deciding in some way that they contributed to the cure of my previous headache. I smiled and resumed my pursuit.

The next stop occurred at the home of Sam Dickerson and his wife, Grace, our school's cook. Both said that they were happy to see me, but when presented with the possibility of buying White Cloverine Salve, each took very little time to reject my sales overture.

After leaving Sam's house, I said, "Good riddance! I never liked Grace's cooking anyway. Besides that, she beat out my mom for the job that belonged rightfully to her."

Mom always told me that Bill Lewis, a distant cousin who dominated the Chinquapin School Board, refused to support his own blood kin due to various political reasons, namely that he and my dad never saw eye to eye on anything.

Sam sent me to see his father, Jordan, who would have bought at least one can if his wife, Tennie, hadn't talked him out of it. I never wanted to chastise a person as badly as I did then, because Tennie failed to realize the impact that her opinion had upon the future of my enterprise.

Frankly, I couldn't understand why all these people failed to take advantage of this great opportunity. Each can of the salve cost only twenty-five cents, but later, as I reflect on the saga, I realized that most of them probably didn't have much more than a quarter to their name and were just too proud to admit it.

After all these unsuccessful sales calls, I became desperate. I was rapidly running out of close neighbors and the apprehension of going into unfamiliar territory, talking to a lot of strangers, sent chills up my spine. But before the dream of that new bow and arrow set dissipated completely, I suddenly hit upon another fantastic idea. If I could persuade Preston Ainsworth, who owned a store near where my Granddad Wright's used to be, to buy the remainder of the salve, he could place the inventory in his store and sell it with a favorable markup. In turn, both of us would benefit handsomely from the proposed contract.

Upon entering Preston's store, I was a little nervous. I approached him cautiously and said, "Preston, I'm selling White Cloverine Salve. Why don't you buy some and sell it for a profit? I only want twenty-five cents a can."

Now, Preston had been a friend of the family for many years, and surely, I predicted, he wouldn't—or couldn't—say no and disappoint me. I saw his wife Annie draw near and whisper something in his ear. I just knew that she had come to my aid and that the next thing I would hear was that they would take all twenty-three cans off my hands.

When Preston spoke, however, all hopes for success were dashed. He informed me that he had bought several cans of White Cloverine Salve years ago. He pointed them out to me. Sure enough, there they were on the upper shelf, gathering dust. He asked me if I had better luck than he'd had. When I mentioned that I had sold but one, he laughed and said, "Well, goldurn boy, you outdid me. I never sold any, marked down even lower than what you're asking."

So much for original ideas! I was distraught and could scarcely hear Preston say as I walked out of the door, "Tell your Mom and Dad hello for us."

Boy, I thought, *does that take nerve or what? He turns me down and expects me to give greetings to my parents.* Added to that, I recollected the earlier occasions when Preston received at least one of the last two dollars that we had at the time in exchange for a gallon of store-bought milk.

I mumbled, "Whatever happened to that old expression: You scratch my back, and I'll scratch yours?" The answer became painfully clear. Needless to say, Preston and Annie occupied the two top spots on my newly created least-favorite list.

I got on my bike and started for home with tears in my eyes. I had to pass each of those houses whose occupants turned away a friend and neighbor in distress. That made matters even worse. When I arrived, Mom realized something was wrong. All I had to show for a morning's sales calls was a measly twenty-five cents. I needed another $5.75, so I became resigned to failure. Mom, however, took pity on my somewhat less-than-fruitful business venture. My eyes brightened, and my spirits soared with eagles when she suggested that maybe she

I NEVER SOLD ANY!
SALVE
GROCERIES
BOOKS
NO SALE
Flour
Flour
SALVE
CALVIN BLASSINGAME

and Dad might buy the remaining lot. She interjected caution, however. I would have to present the idea to Dad, but if he signed on, I was set. She also pointed out that my case would have to be presented with all the ardor and finesse of an experienced trial attorney.

In the tried-and-true fashion of children through the ages, I explained to Dad that Mom had agreed to the family purchase if the terms were acceptable to him. To my surprise, he gave approval. I finally got the $5.75, along with stern advice about becoming involved in matters of this nature in the future. Little did I realize then that this grand total was probably all the money we had in this world, at least what we could lay our hands on. Nevertheless, we always had plenty to eat. The farm provided that, so ready cash was not always a vital issue.

I could hardly wait to mail in the $6.00, and when I did, I expected that the bow and arrow would be received shortly, as had the original salve allotment. I was not yet schooled in the small-print verbiage: Allow four to six weeks for delivery.

Every afternoon I ran from the school bus into the house, hoping that Frank Bates, our mailman, had brought the bow and arrow that very day, but when days turned to weeks, the dreams began to disappear as clouds over a horizon. My mom reminded me constantly that water never boils in a watched pot, but at ten years old, I didn't understand such profound wisdom. Sure enough, though, when I completely forgot about the prize, it finally arrived!

One afternoon I stepped off the bus, walked into the house and into my bedroom. There on the bed lay the thrill of a lifetime. Oh, happy day! I could hardly curb my excitement as I bent the bow and inserted the string into the slots for the first time. With the bow strung, I picked up the single arrow and ran outside to try it out.

The first shot into the empty pasture was a thing of beauty. The arrow sailed straight and true for quite a distance—nothing like the malfunctions of those crude, wobbly, whittled sticks that I usually used. Talk about being keyed up! I eagerly anticipated great hunting ahead, of all those squirrels on the dinner table.

I retrieved the arrow hastily for the second shot, but when I pulled back the bow, the Earth stood still. A sharp snap, a cracking noise broke the silence of a cool spring day. Part of my new treasure fell to the ground and lay at my feet. The bow had splintered beyond repair.

As you might imagine, this situation produced a traumatic effect on a lad who had waited forever only to have the euphoria end so abruptly. While tears turned to anger, I believed that I had been duped into selling a good product in return for a questionable piece of goods. I felt betrayed! How could anyone be so heartless and cruel?

I returned ever so slowly to the house to relay the bad news to Mom, but on the way I gathered my thoughts and eventually turned them into valuable lessons of life. First, a bow and arrow of that quality should not have cost the equivalent of $6.00, plus the incredible sales labor spent in the attempt of unloading all that salve. Second, I was no salesman. If this was what that job was like, I wanted no part of it. I also remembered a stern message relayed by my parents during previous conversations: Nothing in life is free, and if it sounds too good to be true, then it probably is. But after listening to my tale of woe for a few minutes, Mom instilled another important point when she reminded me that because I had become involved in the project on a voluntary basis, I had no one to blame but myself! She also mentioned that word accountability, one that I would not understand the true impact of until later on.

When the dust settled, however, one more thing became abundantly clear—the McKinley family had enough White Cloverine Salve to last for quite a while!

In all fairness to the present and past manufacturers and distributors of White Cloverine Salve, we never contacted them about the broken bow. Had they known about the incident, I'm sure that the item would have been replaced, and everyone, including me, would have been entirely satisfied. But back in those days, it never occurred to any member of my family to bring the matter to anyone's attention. As an additional note, I recently asked Cynthia Millard, the Consumer Affairs Manager of Medtech, the current maker of White Cloverine Salve, to provide me with a complimentary tin of the product. On January 27, 2003, the item was received. My previous complaint of many years has finally been resolved and although never officially created, the invoice has been stamped *Paid-in-Full with Satisfactory Results*.

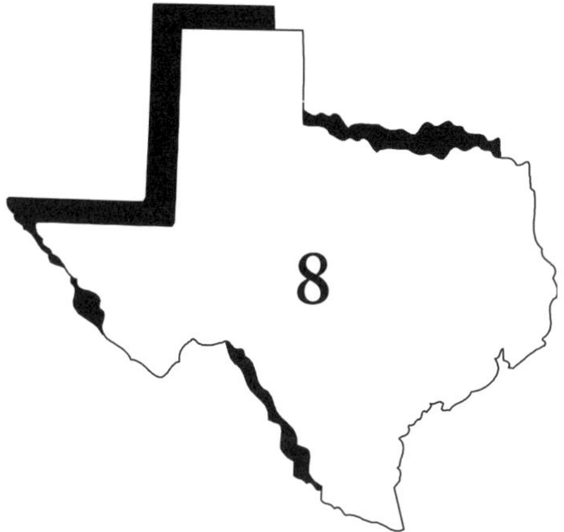

8

THE GREAT CAT MYSTERY

CATS HAVE ALWAYS OCCUPIED A SPECIAL NICHE in my heart. Although dogs accounted for the majority of the family pets, one feline in particular stood above the rest as my all-time favorite. This cat, a large white male with yellow-and-black markings, had been with us for what seemed forever. By appearance, he certainly held no pedigree, and since he just showed up at our doorstep one day, no one in the family knew anything of his past, including his exact age. Dad checked his teeth and concluded that he was probably seven or eight, and for that day and environment, if true, he lived on borrowed time. Mom felt sorry for the old fellow, remarking that he must have been mistreated because he appeared malnourished. So we began to feed and pet him, and then finally, we took him into the family.

When it came time to name him, however, disagreements churned. Dad cast aside my immediate objections, and mandated that we call our new pet Kitty Tom. Even though I was only four years old, I thought the designation redundant and outright pointless. After all, he was a cat—that was no great brainteaser. And he was a tomcat—there was no question about that either. I guess that we followed the same course of logic later on when we got a female cat and named her Kitty Missy. Go figure.

Soon after we adopted Kitty Tom, however, he began to stray and remain away from home for days on end. Dad commented that he must have become romantically entangled with a lady friend, and in the process, misplaced his good senses. I understood none of Dad's reasoning at the time or any of those things that he added about the birds and the bees—and courtship. I questioned why a cat would leave a comfortable habitat and three squares a day to gallivant over the countryside. But Dad soon solved that problem, along with answering my questions, and Kitty Tom became a homebody.

One morning Dad and Uncle Mutt took my friend behind an outbuilding and performed a successful surgical procedure honed after years of dealing with our male hog population. After that, the cat put on considerable mass. Although he topped out at about fifteen pounds, he lost a dominant personality trait. Wanderlust would no longer produce the desire to roam the landscape. Dad noted that he became much too fat to do anything but sleep, but Mom said that nothing around her house would ever go hungry if she had anything to do with it.

Contrary to my father's criticism, however, Kitty Tom pulled his weight around the farm, especially near and inside the barn and corncrib, where field mice posed a continual threat to our crops. As with many of his breed, he often displayed the daily catch at the back doorstep. Although we frequently expressed annoyance with this practice, Kitty Tom seemed not to notice. Who knows what cats think about? I am sure he wanted no more repeat visits behind the barn to alter any part of his remaining physical attributes. I suppose that he also felt that he had better earn his keep and show proof positive; otherwise he would be out of a job and a cushy place to live.

I never remember a time when Kitty Tom wasn't around somewhere or the other. He was as gentle as a lamb, and fortunately, his pleasant disposition saved me from many a scratch that I surely warranted.

As indicated earlier, I viewed cats as special creatures, especially after I heard Dad say that they always landed on their feet, even when falling from great heights. I believed that any animal capable of pulling off that triumph deserved both uncommon consideration and proper investigation. So I set about thinking of ways to analyze Dad's revelation in greater detail.

Recently, I had fallen from the open porch attached to the front of our house, and I certainly did not land on my feet. I wound up lying flat on my back with a tricycle on top. No one had ever seen fit to install a safety railing, and for that reason I went over the side when I rode too close to the edge. Luckily for me, the descent was no more than eighteen to twenty inches, or I would have broken my neck for such callous carelessness. Mom had pointed to that possibility on more than one occasion.

These warnings went in one ear and out the other. I insisted that more important issues required immediate attention, one in particular: how in the heck could a cat set down on all fours when faced with similar peril at even greater heights? So I designed an experiment that would either prove or disprove my dad's theory. I could not simply take his word, no way. The concept would be put to the test and the result, so to speak, would stand on its own merit. I think that you will agree—there is much to be said about this learning process!

One morning, I grabbed an unsuspecting Kitty Tom and walked through the house onto the front porch. As always, he remained motionless in my arms, much like a rag doll, all sprawled out, completely relaxed and limp as a wet dishrag. Although I maintained a firm grip on the subject, I suppose that he thought this would be a morning like most others. The two of us would go into the yard, find a fresh patch of clover, plop down and spend an hour or so looking at the clouds, trying to identify things in the floating masses of white powder puffs that re-sembled rabbits, birds and other creatures. I suspected that he dreamed of good purring ahead while being treated to some pretty steady scratching behind the ears.

When I neared the edge of the porch, however, I threw him in the air, as high as I could, into the yard area. I had picked a landing spot clear of impediments be-cause I didn't want to hurt him in any way. Besides, injury would taint the data. Kitty Tom twisted, turned and then dropped in a big strip of clover, and sure enough—he stood erect, just as Dad predicted.

Please do not instantly start condemning me for mis-treatment of animals. You must give careful consideration to at least two reasons why I should not be brought up on abuse charges. First, a five-year-old kid cannot throw a cat of that size and weight all that far, and second, my mom interceded before any damage occurred.

During his brief time aloft, however, Kitty Tom screamed and howled—obviously he wanted no part of this scientific trial. By the time Mom arrived at the scene to see what caused all the commotion, I had already run down the steps and recaptured him for another test run.

Mom quickly pulled the cat from my arms and began to scold me for such terrible conduct. When she asked me to put myself in his shoes, I thought this a strange perception. After all, anyone in his—or her—right mind knows that cats have paws, and there is no necessity for shoes.

"How would you like to be thrown around like that?" she inquired.

"I wouldn't mind a bit," I bragged, "if I could land on my feet the way that Kitty Tom does. In fact, that would be great!"

How could anyone argue with rationale like that? So Mom resorted to the final remedy. If she caught me repeating this stunt, Dad would hear about it and take more drastic measures to ensure the cat's future safety. I would be the ultimate loser with a sore behind to show for my mischief.

For the time being, I gave in, but days later, a more daring and innovative plan came to mind. As before, the second phase centered on the same, unenthusiastic subject. This time, however, I required ancillary supplies to complete the statistical analysis. I went into the barn and located a nice piece of sturdy string, about fifteen feet in length, that would be placed securely around the cat's upper body. I would then have him run up a tree with the line in tow, and when he had reached the desired height, I would pull like the dickens—and cause him to jump. If he landed on his feet from that extreme altitude, I would be satisfied with the outcome, and no additional inquiries would be necessary. With all the fine points sorted out, I began the maneuver.

Kitty Tom offered no resistance at first, accepting the rigging with usual grace, neither attempting to bite nor scratch me. Then I raised him onto the trunk of a medium-sized oak tree where he promptly attached himself to the bark with those giant, sharp claws that glistened in the sunshine. After a healthy amount of coaxing, he climbed until he reached nearly to the top. All the way up, however, he expressed complete displeasure about his latest predicament by uttering shrill tones, loud enough to get the attention of—you know who!

The twine had plenty of slack, and did not bind him too tightly, I thought. Kitty Tom was in no visible bodily pain, so I had to consider the possibility that he had a fear of heights. I began to feel sorry for him and had just about abandoned the venture altogether when I came up with a backup strategy. If he could not climb down on his own and all else failed, I could drag him out. That would not only help him gain his freedom, but corroborate my research at the same time. Was I not right back to where I started! But again, Mom came to the rescue and intervened.

WHAT EXPERIMENT?

Luckily for Kitty Tom, Mom always seemed to be there when he needed her most. She stood at the kitchen window while doing the morning dishes and she had witnessed part of the proceedings. When she heard the cat's plea for help, she ran to the examination area, jerked the string from my hand and asked what I was up to now.

"Nothing," I explained.

Now I have never quite understood how children seem to learn this particular word nothing long before many others, or how they determine that its use should adequately resolve all serious challenges. Maybe it is a key element of human nature to learn how to fib early on. Who can be sure? Regardless, I gave it my best shot.

But Mom promptly saw through the lame excuse and demanded that I give her a more suitable explanation and fast! When I complied, she failed to see either the humor or the necessity in my scientific actions. I sought immediately to change the subject.

"What if he can't get down?" I asked.

She said that I shouldn't worry about the cat—I had better start paying more attention to my own welfare and learn to stay out of trouble. At that point, I had trounced on the one nerve that Mom had left, so I kept my mouth shut. We continued to look upward into the branches, begging, trying to induce Kitty Tom to take the first step.

But he hung on for dear life, voicing his total annoyance at being placed in that awkward position.

Several minutes later, Mom said that Kitty Tom would rely on his instincts to get to the ground and safety. Now I knew nothing about that word instinct, so I probed further. Mom stated that it was a part of the evolution process and I would just have to take her word for it. I almost asked for more description, but decided against it. After all, Mom was still a little put out by the entire incident.

We walked back into the kitchen and looked from the window. Precisely as forecast, the old cat climbed down from the tree. Before he could make a final breakout, though, Mom removed the line, still attached with one of those square knots that Dad, the World War II naval veteran, showed me how to tie. Kitty Tom was a little nervous, I might add, but he allowed her the freedom to unfasten the noose.

It had been a long morning for everyone concerned, and I concluded that I'd had about all I wanted of this experimentation business. I had other fish to fry. So I promptly entered my room, strapped on my fast-draw holsters that held two cap shooters, walked outside, got on my stick horse and went about my way fighting off imaginary cattle rustlers and bank robbers.

I am certain that Kitty Tom was more than pleased with the outcome. He slyly slipped toward the barn and most probably curled up in his favorite sleeping place to take a morning nap in a much friendlier atmosphere.

About March 1950, Dad decided to earn some extra money, so he packed a few clothes and left for Beaumont where he got a job at the Bethlehem Shipyard. Mom and I remained on the farm, because I still had some time left in the school semester.

My granddad Wright had recently lost his second wife, Emma Marshall, to a lengthy illness and naturally he was down and out. One day he and Mom got to talking and decided that he would come stay with us a while. That might relieve some of his loneliness. Daddy Wright would regain a cook and Mom would have her father around the house to boost her sagging spirits. Besides, she was always afraid of the dark.

So Daddy Wright moved some belongings, including a milk cow—his one remaining farm animal—to our place and before long, all settled into a routine. During the day my grandfather attended his store about two miles down the road and in the late afternoon, he returned to our house to eat supper and spend the night.

Now for reasons outlined below, I presumed that Daddy Wright should provide me with *all* the soft drinks, candy and other goodies that I could possibly desire. As a storeowner, he must have purchased these items at a deep discount. And I deserved special courtesy because

I was his only grandchild in the immediate area—within eight miles anyway.

Each afternoon, I waited patiently for the sound of his jeep, believing that eventually, Daddy Wright might surprise me with a treat. But each arrival turned out the same. He brought nothing except two worn, King Edward cigar boxes, chock-full of paper money and coins.

Daddy Wright always erred on the side of caution, and even in familiar terrain he believed in hiding his money. So after searching the interior of our house for quite a while, he settled upon the ideal spot. He bent down, removed the bottom panel from the Servel, our butane-powered refrigerator, pushed the cigar boxes underneath and reattached the cover. He said that this represented the perfect place; no one would ever think to look there.

My grandfather never kept his money out in the open because he said that it would pose an unnecessary enticement to steal. He concluded that if the wrong people saw it, they might knock us in the head, slit our throats from ear to ear and make off with his loot. I always worried about that observation, and felt uneasy about the funds stored in our household, even on a temporary basis.

"Oh well," I observed, "that's something new to ponder over."

Soon thereafter, a pattern developed and continued Monday through Saturday, just like clockwork. My grandfather ate and slept, came and went, and I felt slighted. Where were my personal benefits in this arrangement? Finally, I'd had all that I could possibly withstand. Everyone has limits, even a six-year-old kid. Daddy Wright was getting free room and board, so I determined that he should be a little more generous. It was time for him to share some of that candy, or better still, a big old Moon Pie and a Royal Crown Cola. Why I did not come out and ask him directly is beyond me, but I did the next best thing. I fell back on pouting to get my way.

After several days of my avoiding him completely, our guest began to wonder about the silent treatment. He looked toward Mom and quizzed, "Is the boy sick or something?"

"No," she explained. "He's just a little hurt. You know how Fred Barry is. He wears his feelings on his sleeve. He would feel much better, though, if you brought him a piece of candy every now and then."

The following afternoon, I almost didn't know how to react when Daddy Wright asked me to search his khaki shirt pocket, which offered up one of those mouth-watering Hershey bars, the kind with those little blocks designed for bite-sized consumption. My ploy worked! Optimism kicked into high gear, and all signs pointed to a good start on mending our relationship. Had my grandfather begun a tradition that would last indefinitely?

I do need to add for the record that according to my way of thinking, he never brought a sufficient quantity. I never got two and certainly never got three, but only one candy bar at a time! I guess that he didn't want to spoil me too much.

Regardless of the number, however, Daddy Wright became my new best friend. I met him at the door each evening with hands outstretched. He gave that robust laugh and remarked that I was going to eat up all his profits. I didn't take his comment seriously at first, but I found out a few days later that he meant every word of it. Much to my regret, he stopped bringing the sweets and resumed his usual stance on strict and austere supply-side economics.

During the interim, Dad had come home at every opportunity, but his visits lasted only a day or two at the most. About the end of May, Mom and I were surprised one afternoon when Uncle Walter Crocker and his family drove up unexpectedly, with Dad as a passenger. Dad got out and invited everyone to come in. My relatives' visit appeared a little peculiar, but by the next morning, I understood the motive.

Uncle Walter was a schoolteacher. Most summers, he usually attended Stephen F. Austin College in nearby

Nacogdoches, where he continued studying for a Master's degree in education. This time, he brought my aunt and their son along to keep him company. He explained that the family residence in Beaumont would be vacant for about six weeks. He allowed Dad to use it and hoped that Mom and I would be invited to tag along for the same time period.

At first, everyone voiced overwhelming approval. But Mom soon balked and asked what would happen to Papa. Dad remarked that the old man could take care of himself; he had done so before and he could certainly do it again. Mom argued convincingly that Daddy Wright had just settled in and that he had gone to a lot of trouble in moving his cow to our pasture. My grandfather quickly put an end to the disagreement and said that he didn't want to cause any internal conflicts. He suggested that we take Uncle Walter up on his proposition.

With everything set, the Crocker family left for Nacogdoches the following morning, and we started packing a few things to take with us to Beaumont. Daddy Wright went to his house and said that he would come back later for the cow. Mom could not get this off her mind and always felt guilty about leaving her dad by himself, so close after the untimely death of his wife. Later, she confided to me that it was one of the more painful decisions that she had ever made.

Excitedly, I asked Dad how we were going to transport Kitty Tom, but I was shocked to hear that he would not be among the baggage. Dad stated that he would be much happier in his own surroundings. After all, he was not a city dweller. He said that the cat would go stark, raving crazy if he rode in the car, and he would probably jump out somewhere along the way. I tried to refute the point, but I fought a losing battle. When I reiterated that Uncle Walter had a horse barn where Kitty Tom could put up for the short term, Dad swiftly vetoed that motion and warned that I leave well enough alone.

On Sunday morning, Random Hardy, one of our friends, came by the house and said that he would watch after the cat.

"Now how can he do that?" I asked. "He lives up the road at least four miles or so."

Dad replied that because Kitty Tom was extremely resourceful, everything would be fine.

I repeated the question. "Pray tell, how can Random keep his word living so far away?"

Random attempted, without much success, to assure me that he would do exactly as promised. I had nothing to worry about.

Before leaving for Beaumont, I walked to the barn, found Kitty Tom, made my peace and determined that I would most likely never set eyes on him again, not in this life anyway. Almost blinded by tears, I returned to the house with the most terrible empty feeling ever experienced. I was leaving a friend behind. I knew now how Mom must have felt.

Neither the trip nor the stay measured up to my expectations. During the next few weeks, my mind constantly drifted toward the home place. Concentration on anything else became an impossible task. I continued to be troubled about the unknown condition of Kitty Tom, over a hundred miles away. I was ecstatic when Dad returned from work one afternoon about five weeks later and said that his job was finished. We were going home, back to Chinquapin.

The next day, we pulled up to the front of the house, which appeared extremely dismal. The lawn, or what was left of it, had overgrown with weeds and Johnson grass. It was strangely quiet. I jumped from the car and started looking for the cat, but he was nowhere in sight. I concluded that since we had taken a powder, he must have left for more favorable surroundings. After the captain deserts, why should any self-respecting sailor stay with a sinking ship?

I went back into the house and blurted, "That's just what I expected! Kitty Tom is gone! Random lied, and I'm out of a cat. You just can't trust anybody nowadays."

Dad smiled and suggested that I keep the faith. I should dig deep and resist the temptation of being so negative. He reminded me about those stories of Lassie and how she found her way across great expanses to be reunited with loved ones. He added that cats are much more cunning and resilient and are better able to fend for themselves than dogs. So if Lassie could do it, Dad alleged, Kitty Tom could do it better. He concluded that I should maintain my patience and stay the course; he truly believed that the cat would reappear.

"No way," I rebutted. "This is not going to happen. We've been gone for too long and the trail has grown cold by now. He will never find his way back. Besides, everybody keeps talking about him being lost. He may well be pushing up daisies!"

About ten days passed and Kitty Tom did not materialize. Although I had not completely given up hope, I was still more than a little incensed by the current state of affairs. One morning I got up reluctantly. With mixed feelings, I busied myself planning the daily activities that included playing cowboys and Indians, throwing in a little Tarzan for good measure.

We had just sat down to have breakfast when someone knocked on the door. Random dropped by, or so he said, to check on the family and to see if we needed anything. But then he left in an awful big hurry. He didn't stay long enough to have a cup of Mom's hot coffee. That was irregular, because I knew how Random loved coffee.

After eating, I walked into the back yard and into the side pasture. A powerful and constant meowing that came from the direction of the hilltop broke the silence of the morning air. I looked toward the caterwauling and could not believe my eyes. I saw a cat that resembled mine, running full tilt toward me. As it drew nearer, I realized that it was Kitty Tom.

I snatched him up, ran into the house and admitted to Dad that he was right after all. Dad cast a wink in Mom's direction, but I didn't think much about it at the time. Kitty Tom had returned—that was the important thing. I soon forgot about the incident and turned my attention to preparing for the new school year. Hey, I was going into the second grade.

During a conversation years later, I asked Dad about that curious set of circumstances. I speculated where the cat may have been for those five or so weeks. How did Kitty Tom know that we were back, and why did he choose that particular morning to make his long-awaited entrance?

From out of the blue, Dad uttered a strange response. He said, "Oh, I never told you!"

"Told me what?" I asked.

He explained that Random came by the house the very next day after we had left for Beaumont. Due to my affection and serious concern for the cat's well-being, he picked up the temporary cast-off and carried him home, where he and Alma catered to his every need with daily servings of warm milk and all the extras. Random said that the old fellow never had it so good. When Random heard that we were in the neighborhood, he drove past and turned the cat loose on the other side of the hill that overlooked our house. Then he retraced his steps, stopped briefly and left before Kitty Tom could announce his presence.

"Son of a gun," I asserted. "Look at all the time I spent worrying and fretting over him, believing that he would starve to death, and now you tell me this. Why didn't you say something earlier?"

Dad said that he didn't want to mention it, fearing that it would spoil the surprise reunion. Afterward he chose not to because I told everyone that I owned a cat that used exceptional talents to divine our proximity and find his way home. Dad said that by that time he didn't want to burst my bubble, so he kept silent.

Kitty Tom stayed with us for another two years, until he came up missing. If someone had stolen him, I believed that he would eventually escape and turn up as before. This time, however, the outcome was different. I hoped then, as I still do today, that he didn't come to any harm. He earned the highest respect and certainly deserved a better fate.

We should be careful to get out of an experience only the wisdom that is in it—and stop there; lest we be like the cat that sits down on a hot stove-lid. She will never sit down on a hot stove-lid again—and that is well; but also she will never sit down on a cold one anymore.

—Mark Twain

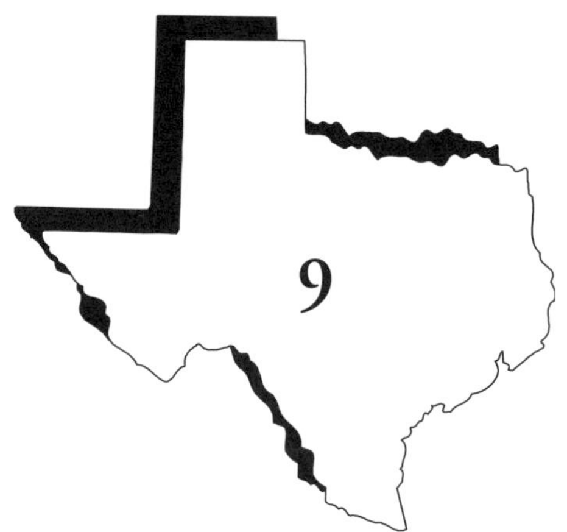

LESSON IN HONESTY

IMMEDIATELY BEFORE THE BEGINNING OF MY SEC-ond-grade school year during 1950, Dad announced that we were going to San Augustine to purchase some clothes and other supplies. Most children of that era and background did not receive new school apparel other than at the start of a school year. Those garments were expected to last for a full nine months, so when we came home from school, we took off the school duds and replaced them with play attire, usually the tattered ones that remained from previous terms.

My clothes usually came in the form of underwear, socks, shoes and three pairs of striped overalls. Mother still supplied the inventory of homemade shirts, but what really excited me this year was that I was going to get cowboy boots and my first real pair of blue jeans. Those striped overalls were finally being retired.

We didn't have a car, and since San Augustine was over eight miles away, Dad and I caught a ride into town with a distant relative and neighbor, Clyde Lewis. At the time, Clyde owned a beat-up Chrysler of some kind, which had a distinctive appearance. There wasn't another like it in the county, as far as we knew.

I remember that particular Saturday morning well. I climbed into the back with my clean, crisp overalls and freshly ironed shirt, fighting to beat the grime off the seat in order to find a place to hunker without getting too filthy. It was hot, and the windows were rolled down. Dust from the red-dirt road, parched by the summer sun, filled the interior, making it extremely difficult for me to catch a breath of fresh air.

When we arrived in town, Clyde drove around for a spell. He couldn't find the parking place that he wanted, so he dropped Dad and me in front of the dry-goods store. He informed us that when we were through with our business affairs, we could place our goods in his car, which would be parked somewhere near the courthouse square. The fact that we had no key caused no special difficulty, because auto security was unimportant in those days. Besides, the trunk lock on Clyde's car hadn't worked in ages.

At that time, I considered that the three most important things in life—with the exception of my parents and grandparents—were my dog and cat and the thrill of buying those new blue jeans and cowboy boots. My present footwear, literally worn to a frazzle, had been scuffed by a great deal of kneeling, sliding and playing marbles on the schoolyard, so it was time for a replacement.

After what seemed like hours of searching, Dad and I found the perfect pair of boots. These beauties, which were a red, almost crimson, color with black tops, were the most impressive things that I had ever seen. My heart raced with anticipation at the thought of wearing them to school for the first time. Surely I would be the envy of every boy on campus, especially when they saw me with those new blue jeans.

That day I got four pairs of Wranglers and that excited me even more. The clerk at Clark and Downs Dry Goods wrapped the purchases and tied a string around everything to make handling the bulky packages much easier.

Dad and I walked to the vicinity of the courthouse square and searched for Clyde's car. It made no sense to lug our bundles around all day, so we decided to do as our good neighbor suggested and store them in the trunk. Clyde had found a parking spot just where he'd indicated.

After opening the trunk, Dad moved a bunch of junk around—Clyde was not very tidy—and placed the parcels inside. We left then to visit my Uncle Paul Wright, who owned a grocery store just across the street. Clyde said that he would look us up when he got ready to head for home.

Uncle Paul had left the premises to run an errand, so we walked around town for a couple of hours. Dad said that we didn't have time to go to the show—the term used to describe the Augus Theater—that day, so he took me to Stripling's Drug Store, where I enjoyed a huge bowl of vanilla ice cream, my favorite. After that, I admired the new toys at the Western Auto and the Five and Dime.

Clyde finally met us on the street and asked if we were ready to go. With our business concluded, we decided to strike out for Chinquapin. By the time we reached the car, he had moved it from the original location, but no matter, we got in and left.

When we pulled in at home, Dad and I got out. Clyde remained in the car and left the motor running. We opened the trunk to retrieve the packages, but to our amazement and complete shock, they weren't there. Someone had stolen my new clothes—and my heavens, the boots were gone as well! Clyde expressed sympathy about the incident and sped away in a cloud of dust, leaving Dad and me to wonder about the identity of the

WHERE'S MY STUFF?

rotten, no-good, sorry, low-down culprit who had stooped so low to effect the most hideous crime known to humanity.

Dad assured me, however, that we would return to San Augustine the very next Saturday and replace all the stolen goods. That didn't help much at the time, because I just knew that I would never find another pair of boots that I liked. But things turned around, Dad kept his word, and on the following Saturday, everything, including identical boots, was replaced. We chalked up the whole thing to experience and promptly forgot about it.

About two months later, Dad, Mom and I were seated on the front porch one late afternoon when we saw Clyde's car coming down the road from the direction of San Augustine. That was unusual, because we hadn't seen him pass earlier, and besides, he usually asked if we wanted to go into town or whether we needed anything. We did notice, however, that as the car came nearer, an old black man sat behind the wheel. Maybe Clyde had sold his car...but we hadn't heard anything about that either. Something strange was going on.

The old man stopped in front of the house, killed the motor, got out slowly and walked through the gate and up to where we sat. He inquired of my dad, "Are you Mista Fred?"

Dad answered in the affirmative and asked how he could help.

"Well, suh," the old man continued, "I jus' might have somethin' that belongs to you and yo boy. I found it a while back while I was lookin' in my turtle hull for a jack." For those of you who may not know, "turtle hull" is the country vernacular for an auto trunk.

The family was puzzled by the old man's statement, but the answer soon revealed itself as he walked to his car, opened the trunk and removed the lost packages that contained my school clothes and red cowboy boots. The conversation turned to the similarity of the old man's car with Clyde's, including the fact that both trunk locks were defective. Mother fixed him a cup of coffee, and we all sat around discussing this out-of-the-ordinary situation. Dad thanked him for his trouble, especially for returning the misplaced items to the rightful owners.

When the old gentleman left, my parents used the episode to demonstrate the fact that honesty pays. That example remains vivid in my memory. It is as true now as it was way back then. Everyone should realize that regardless of skin color, religious beliefs, political affiliations or all those other things that we discuss in today's much-divided society, integrity and goodness still exist. But for me, as I recall the outward appearances of those crusty, beat-up Chrysler automobiles, the most valuable lesson of all is neither to form conclusions too hastily, nor to judge a book—or a car for that matter—by its cover.

128

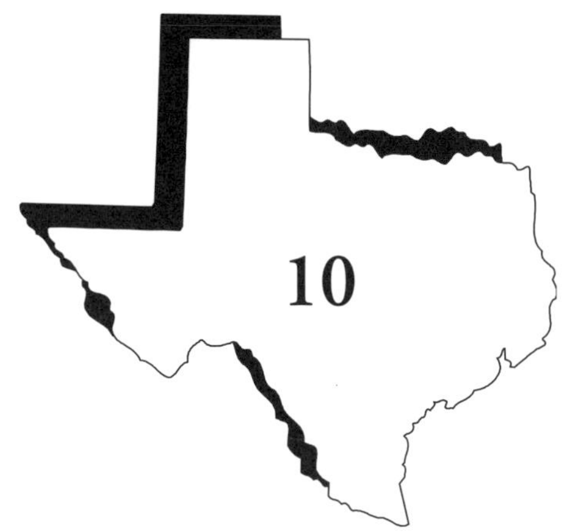

10

MORE TRIALS AND TRIBULATIONS

THE 1950 SCHOOL YEAR BEGAN TRAUMATICALLY with the perceived theft of my school duds and cowboy boots, but things settled down after the first days of class. Around the middle of September, however, a more serious problem developed. I began to slur my words, and as November neared, so did my full-blown case of stuttering.

Now I knew all too well about that affliction—my uncle Burrell Wright had been doing it for years. I asked Mom several times why he talked like that. She said that she had no idea, but that he had stuttered ever since he was a kid. When I asked why his parents never took him to see a doctor and seek out a cure, she didn't have any opinion on that either, other than they were just poor country folk who just dealt with and accepted those things.

As with previous concerns, I thought continually about the stuttering puzzle and lay awake many a night wondering whether this would be the scourge of a lifetime. Mom asked me not to worry about it and pointed out that the problem would take care of itself. I remained skeptical for just cause.

The teachers decided to put on a school play that particular Thanksgiving season. Of course the theme contained the expected characters of pilgrims, Indians and turkeys, but this one carried a little different twist. Our play included a white rabbit, and I won that coveted part. I don't remember how my role fit into the standard holiday tradition, but regardless, I was cast as the lone, designated rabbit with a rather large speaking part.

Mrs. Collins, my second-grade teacher, sent word to Mom and asked her to fabricate an appropriate costume for me. She also enclosed the dialogue and requested that Mom make sure that I learn my part well.

As I said earlier, Mom was a former teacher. I always thought that she would have been an excellent drill sergeant at some military boot camp, because she believed that persistent repetition was the answer to any learning obstacle. Early on, she decided that her only son would not only memorize his lines quickly, he would also deliver them in a fashion that would most certainly turn veteran actors green with envy. So we began the campaign!

During numerous rehearsals both at home and school, however, my stuttering became worse, until finally I had just about given up. I arrived home from class one afternoon and promptly announced that I was not going to be able to shoulder my latest assignment. Mrs. Collins would just have to find someone else to carry the play; some other kid would have to step up to the plate and perform the part of the white rabbit.

Mom, never one to give up on a project very quickly, decided on a plan. She held no appreciation whatsoever for those who squandered time and energy without first gaining some benefit in the process. Mom had invested a lot of effort, and she was not about to fold the tent and quit now.

She had already begun sewing the rabbit suit, made from an old pair of bleached long johns. To make the garb more realistic, she attached a puffy while tail to the now sewn-shut back-door flap. That looked okay, but I was not overly impressed with the appearance of the bunny feet or the early stages of the headgear. Although I expressed a few doubts about the authenticity of the latest additions, the tailoring operation continued under my watchful eye. After all, if the project strayed too far from center, I could exercise certain rights and demand corrective action. If Mom failed to follow my suggestions at that point, I would have no choice but to wield the big stick—the final veto authority.

So with all things considered, I accepted Mom's rendition as a limited success, but with reservations. However when I saw those long, pink ears that flopped over and draped past my shoulders, differences of opinion about design and quality control soon developed. I argued that the ears should stand erect, but Mom countered that she couldn't do any better. Besides, no one would ever notice.

"Baloney," I complained. "Those things look awful, and I'm not going to wear them or that stupid-looking suit! Another thing, I'm not going to be in that old play either."

I had already concluded that if I donned this outfit in the public arena and began my speaking part with a bunch of stuttering, I would become the laughingstock of the campus, not to mention the rest of the community. I had enough problems already; I certainly didn't need to seek out any new ones. My plate was full, and I wanted no part of the Thanksgiving play. And too, I had some exposure to those popular immortal words of wisdom: It is better to be silent and be thought a fool than to speak and remove all doubt. This expression, in my estimation, summed up the entire affair.

AIN'T GONNA WEAR THIS RABBIT SUIT!

Mom soon tired of my insolence and unhelpful attitude. She gave me one of her patented looks and suggested that I should be quiet. When I began to mutter something under my breath, she issued stern advice that I leave well enough alone. With complete dissatisfaction, I complied after finally realizing that my best offensive thrust had neither penetrated, nor even placed a small dent in her defenses. I had to now face the reality of defeat on both fronts. Not only had I failed to persuade her to reconstruct those pitiful excuses for ears, but she also refused to allow me to withdraw from the part that would surely generate a lot of ribbing from my classmates, considering that I would probably get all tangled up in the verbiage. Talk about adding insult to injury!

But all was not lost—hope springs eternal. As I said, Mom had a plan. With pencil and paper in hand, she sat at the dining room table and began rewriting my individual lines within the script. She inserted those things called synonyms, which of course I had never heard of.

When I complained that my teachers would never accept such foolishness, she said, "Don't worry. I've got that covered too."

So Mom continued the process. With skilled precision, she would give me a word to replace one that I could not pronounce without going into my stuttering routine. She then directed me to repeat the new word several times, until I assured her that I could carry on without interruption. After what seemed several hours, we were set. One important detail remained, however—another cleverly constructed note to the teacher. Mom patiently informed Mrs. Collins that she had taken matters into her own hands. Her only son could not vocalize many of the words in the original dialogue, so she had taken care of it.

I was a little embarrassed about the whole experience and delayed delivering the note to the teacher for as long as possible. But I did what was expected of me, and things worked out. The play went off without a hitch, and I was rather proud of my performance. I even got two or three compliments on my rabbit suit. Once again, Mom saved the day.

During the early part of 1951, my speech returned to normal. Recently I learned that even though no one has ever identified the actual cause of stuttering, most clinicians agree that it is definitely not associated with emotional trauma or fear. Many propose that it most probably lies in the area of child development, but when it comes to the question of cure, these same professionals remain divided. The Stuttering Foundation of America, however, presents one of the most accepted methods used to treat the stuttering disorder. It claims that early intervention is the best form of combat.

As with the experts, we never knew what prompted my bout with the riddle that afflicts some three million Americans, and we never quite understood why my stuttering stopped as quickly as it began. Perhaps unknowingly, Mom had adopted and applied the early intervention technique when she took it on herself to change the words in that long-forgotten scenario. Whatever the reason, Mom was right, as usual. I grew out of it.

Later that same year, I began to notice a definite change in my fingers. Sure, I was growing, and my fingers were getting longer and larger. But all of a sudden, rough spots appeared, and before I knew it, small growths seemed to pop up everywhere. Dad quickly diagnosed the situation and concluded that I had a bunch of seed warts. Without question, I knew what seeds were, but I had no experience with warts. As a resident of the farming community, we used seeds to plant corn, watermelons, cotton and such. I knew also that seeds spouted and grew, but I was slow to determine how the two words seed and warts fit together in the big picture.

My folks tried various home medications to halt the spread of those funny-looking little bumps, but nothing worked. Finally I suggested using the exalted White Cloverine Salve, recalling the many cures claimed by the manufacturer. But when that product failed unexpectedly, I became seriously alarmed and feared the worst. I had good reason. On many a hot summer night, I had heard those Baptist preachers talk about the sufferings of lepers, and how they were misunderstood and ill-treated by their fellowman. Was this how that particular problem began, with a bunch of seed warts?

"Surely," I said to Dad, "these things will grow bigger and eventually cover every inch of skin on my whole body. Soon I will become an outcast of society."

Dad smiled, patted my shoulder and told me not to worry so much. He also said that he would think on it. But he did assure me of one thing: I did not have a case of the leprosy. I must say, that took quite a load off my mind.

Later at school, Harold, Lee Allen and the rest of my buddies resolved that I must have touched a frog. After all, folks throughout millennia have known that frogs are the basic cause of warts. But I would not accept such rubbish because I had no memory of ever playing with one of those rascals. Besides, there wasn't enough water around our property to attract a frog of the size necessary to produce the quantity of seed warts found on my fingers. "Boy, that would take a whopper!" I said.

Mom and Dad wearied of my constant whining about the wart situation. So Dad got personally involved and called for the services of an outside professional consultant. One morning, at about 10 o'clock, George Ford and his wife, Tera, whom we called Teet, arrived at our front door. Mom invited them to come in, and as usual, all enjoyed a good cup of coffee. But why the visit? To my knowledge the couple, who lived near Daddy Wright, had never set foot in our house before, so I thought this peculiar. George asked me to come to his side and extend my hands for closer inspection. He felt of my fingers and said, "I see. Well, we'll just have to do somethin' about that."

George lived down the road a few miles. I'd heard once that he was a World War I veteran, but that was about all I knew of him. In fact, I never knew if he had a job or how he supported himself and the family, unless by farming. But this morning I was about to discover something new about him—something that I never dreamed of!

I trembled a bit and asked what he was doing. George looked toward Dad and then toward me and said, "I'm a fixin' to get rid of your warts."

"How are you going to do that?" I asked.

I quickly remembered how Dad and others got rid of long horns on our cattle, and I once saw Dad and Uncle Mutt rid a dog of his tail. Soon afterwards, we changed the dog's name to fit his new state—Bob.

"Surely," I said to George, "you're not going to cut them off!"

"No," he replied, "Nothing that drastic. Just wait and be patient."

George directed that all spectators leave the room and when he and I were alone, he asked me to turn my head and close my eyes. I was more than a little fearful about the current goings on, but I had no control of the situation. Before Dad walked out of the living room to the front porch, he advised me to be quiet, listen and follow all directions to the letter.

So I did. George began to rub my fingers gently and murmur something—mumbo-jumbo, more than likely—that I could not understand. He used none of the usual smelly ointments, liniments or common household salves, including the cool, clover-scented White Cloverine brand, but I felt heat being generated just the same! I wanted naturally to sneak a peek, but I resisted. In about two minutes, George announced that he was through with the application. Before I could open my eyes, however, I should pay extreme attention to the most crucial detail in the entire procedure: I could not lay eyes on my fingers and hands for six weeks. I should forget that either existed.

"Six weeks," I scoffed. "Why six weeks? How in the world can a person go for that long without looking at his hands? That's much easier said than done."

"Try your best," he cautioned, "but if you do and have a relapse, I'll have to repeat the treatment. I will guarantee one thing. If you do as I say, the warts will disappear and you will never again be faced with them."

No way, I thought. *This is the most half-witted thing that I've ever heard or witnessed.*

About that time, Dad reentered the living room where he reiterated George's prescription for healing. Soon the neighbors departed, and I was left with the delicate task of spending six weeks without so much as a quick glance at the ends of my arms.

I tried to get my mind off the situation, but from time to time, I had to use a pencil and prepare homework. But as George counseled, I did the best that I could. I'm not sure how much time had passed, but one day, I forgot about the instructions and inadvertently cast a long look at my fingers and hands. To my astonishment, the warts had vanished.

I ran to Mom and Dad with this revelation, and each seemed to be as thrilled as I was. Amid much speculation, both swore on a stack of Bibles that they had no idea how George Ford accomplished this fantastic miracle. I tried to make sense of it all. I had seen Noble Garrett use a willow stick and locate water in the most unlikely of all places. I had previously determined that Noble possessed some type of special energy and even labeled him as a medicine man, descended from some lost and forgotten Indian tribe.

For quick analysis, I fell back on another precedent. I knew that Gladys Dickerson boiled roots and dispensed homemade potions amongst the area residents. She healed a host of abnormalities and medically related stresses, but her specialty lay in the discipline of pain management associated with bad teeth and gums, described by modern dentistry as periodontal disease. I quickly eliminated Gladys from the mix of possibilities.

Because of his superior ability, however, I elevated George Ford to a newly created and loftier position. He had personally rid me of warts, and no scientific justification was at hand. Most probably, no one in our small community had ever heard about—much less used—salicylic acid and cantharidin, present-day applications employed to successfully treat the problem.

I entertained no doubt that George Ford possessed mystic powers, but to what degree? Later, when I read about the Druid priesthood, I wondered whether their ancient abilities were really lost, or might they have been passed to recent generations, and eventually to George Ford?

I also knew that my granddad Wright held membership in the Masonic Lodge, and long before Dad's initiation into the same brotherhood, I heard him jest about those secret handshakes, signs, passwords and rituals. If George Ford held to the same tenets, maybe he used some of that fraternity's old-time technology to conquer the wart infestation. This outside chance remained until 1984, when I finally dispelled all childish notions. That's the year that I became a Mason and discovered that none of my new brethren professed to have such magical capabilities.

Perhaps one could offer another solution. As a child, I listened to a multitude of Baptist ministers stand at the pulpit of the small Chinquapin Church and preach hellfire and brimstone. Sparing no detail, they traced the story of Moses and how the Lord Jehovah unleashed terrible plagues on the Egyptian people because the Pharaoh refused to free the children of Israel. With that religious setting in mind, I contemplated that I was being punished for personal sins and transgressions, and as a result, I was forced to endure my own dose of pestilence. When George Ford came to my aid, however, he must have dialed the direct line to Divine Providence, who answered a simple prayer and allowed a mortal to deliver the antidote.

But regardless of the formula, my warts were gone, and as promised, they never returned. Once I asked my friend and neighbor how he did it. He smiled and replied, "It's a secret, and I can't tell you."

Believe it or not, the experts contend that nail biting is the principal cause of seed warts, brought on by a viral infection that incubates in the broken skin. Maybe during his initial examination of my fingers, George Ford found that I was a nail biter of the highest rank. As a student, he could have previously read medical journals or other periodicals and ingeniously applied the understanding to my particular case. I did refrain from biting my fingernails during that six-week or so hiatus, and maybe that's the answer to the medical mystery. Yet according to the American Academy of Dermatology, warts can disappear without any treatment whatsoever.

I have finally come to recognize that perhaps no credible explanation ever existed. Who really knows for sure? But I did find out one thing for certain. George Ford had the gift, and mine was but one success story documented among the many in and around the vicinity of Chinquapin.

As a camel beareth labor, and heat, and hunger, and thirst, through deserts of sand, and fainteth not; so the fortitude of a man shall sustain him through all perils.

—Akhenaton

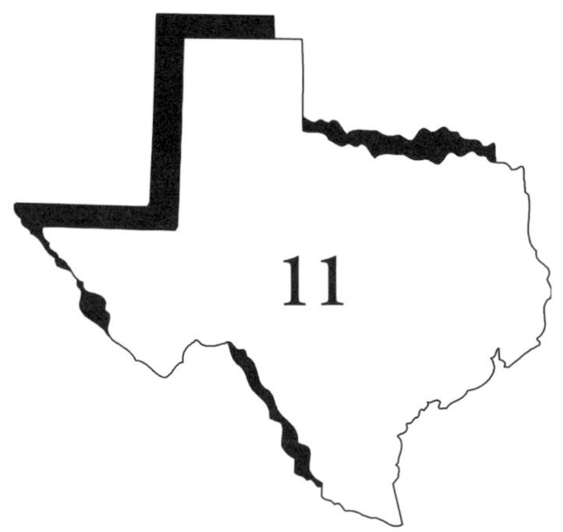

RODEO BOUND

MANY MEMBERS OF MY FAMILY HAVE LONG been associated with one of the real passion sports of the Old West. As long as I could remember, Dad and I accompanied my uncle Jess Simmons and his son, Pete, to witness the spectacles, chills, spills and thrills of rodeos held in various arenas located in nearby San Augustine and Jasper, Texas. After much thought about my future vocational prospects, I assumed that the love of rodeos was in my blood. I yearned to follow in the footsteps of my cousin, Durwood, and another relative by marriage, Pascal Dickerson.

Durwood made quite a name for himself on the regional circuit as a bull rider supreme. Although Pascal stuck primarily within the sphere of calf roping, he also became well known for his specialty. Both were extremely good, but when comparing the two, Durwood remained my greater idol. His father, Walter Crocker, always said that he put him on horseback when he was a baby, and after growing up around horses and cattle, Durwood made the transition to the professional rodeo business with ease. Furthermore, he talked, acted and looked every bit the true cowboy, and with bowed legs from sitting astride a saddle most of his life, he walked as a real Texan. Considering this enormous influence, I supposed that fortune ordained me to opt for the sport of bull riding.

Mom, always the realist, never shirked from pointing out the hazards of my chosen profession. She reminded me constantly that I was only a youngster, and that a seven- or eight-year-old kid had no business thinking about such dangerous things. She suggested that I be content within the safe confines of academia, and as expected, I countered with great arguments. I advised her that her own beloved sister Bertha allowed her son to ride bulls and horses, and that I should be treated no differently. Discrimination would not be tolerated! Even though Mom won out in the interim, I would have my day.

Every time Pascal came to visit, he discussed his most current rodeo experience, and naturally, those stories renewed my desires. Pascal always carried a saddle and other related equipment in his car or truck, and once he let me use his rope to sharpen my skills on the numerous fence posts that circled our house.

After Dad purchased Joe, I began to flesh out my plans. But with a narrow escape from death by that cantankerous Brahma, I decided that I should wait a while before attempting to ride a bull of his size and strength. When Dad bought additional cows and calves, however, I determined that it was time to bring up the issue once more.

Now I had never persuaded Dad that I should ride bulls either. Without question, he knew the sport to be deadly, and he had plans for me to go to college, get married, produce grandchildren, live to be a ripe old age and die quietly in my sleep, *without* my boots on. No matter how hard I begged, he never allowed me to straddle the back of one of those Brahma calves, at least for the time being.

One hot, summer afternoon, Pascal came by the house. He and Dad walked into the front pasture, admiring the hay crop and the recently acquired cattle in the distance. While following along, I realized that this would be the best opportunity to make my case.

I asked, "Hey, Pascal, have you been doing any rodeoing lately?"

"Sure have," he replied. "Why?"

"Well," I stated, "I've been thinking about going into the bull-riding business some day, and I thought that perhaps I could practice on one of our Brahma heifers."

Pascal winked at Dad, and when he smiled, I saw promise for the first time. Dad looked at me and then toward our visitor. "Pack, I guess that this boy will never be happy until he makes an attempt. What do you think?"

Pascal nodded and responded, "There's no time like the present. I have a rope in my truck. Let's go back to the house, get it and catch one of these calves. We'll see what kind of stuff the boy has."

Dad agreed and at that very moment, I felt as if God had anointed me with special powers. I walked tall and proud alongside the two grownups as we returned to the truck parked in front. With the rite of passage so near at hand, I could now finally prove my manhood to all spectators. Filled with unbridled exuberance, I ran into the house and announced the historic occasion to my mother, who took the news with a strong hint of cynicism.

No matter, this would be the day remembered throughout the annals of time immemorial. I imagined that years later, when I was sitting at the pinnacle of professional greatness, I would look back on this experience as the career-launching ride. I saw myself climbing onto the back of that Brahma calf, placing my hand underneath the surcingle that surrounded the animal's midsection, and then yelling, "Turn her loose!" Minutes later, everyone, including my mom would congratulate me on the most fantastic ride ever witnessed by mankind. They would marvel at my style and make comments like "I was sure wrong about you boy. I know genius when I see it, and you have more raw talent than anyone I've ever observed at such a young age."

Reality finally set in when Mom walked out of the house into the yard and made a strange commentary, "Go ahead and break your neck! You'll never be happy until you try it."

I attempted to convince her that everything would be okay. "Just wait," I said, "I'll show you!"

While I daydreamed, Dad and Pascal succeeded in roping a female calf and busied themselves attaching the riding gear. They dragged the terrorized animal to an area near the house and hollered for me to hurry. Soon I stood near destiny with all the confidence of a champion gladiator, dressed in crisp, starched and ironed blue jeans, a western shirt, cowboy boots and the trademark western hat.

Pascal, the experienced one, helped me onto the back of the Brahma, which by now was even more scared out of her wits. The veteran issued instructions about keeping my head high and my eyes wide open. I should also hold the surcingle as tightly as possible with the left hand—while waving the other—and it would be ever better still if I used my hat to spur the animal to create more pronounced movements learned eventually by veteran stock. He explained how this maneuver pleased the judges into awarding more points for individual performances. When I expressed that I understood, he told Dad to stand back and asked if I was ready.

"I've been ready! Let her rip."

With that, he slapped the calf on the rear, and away we went. From the get-go, things did not proceed as I originally planned. During real rodeos, Brahma bulls bucked and twisted as they ran from the chutes. That's what I expected! But this calf, obviously, had never been involved in real competition. She was as much a novice as I was.

The calf took off like a rocket toward the fence. She headed in the direction of the pasture, where the remainder of the cattle seemed to have stopped eating long enough to watch the current entertainment. Within a blink of an eye, the Brahma left the ground, bounded over the fence like a yearling deer, ran to the pond and paused to recuperate from all the excitement.

I, on the other hand, failed to make the trip. I must have let loose of the rope in the tense situation because I landed squarely on my back. Gasping for air, I lay there in misery, while recalling Mom's quote, "Go ahead and break your neck!"

Surely this has come to pass, I thought. *I'll never be able to walk again.*

BAD CAREER
CHOICE!

As my all-too-brief life passed before me, I remained in the horizontal position seemingly for hours, trembling at the hint of fatal injury. With renewed breath, however, came the tears and screams about my self-diagnosed prognosis, and soon, I began to pass blame and judgment. I expressed anger and earnestly questioned why Mom and Dad would let their only child take such a serious risk. They should have known better than to listen to Pascal Dickerson. What were they trying to do, maim me for life?

When everyone arrived at my side and saw that I was all right, I became embarrassed by my recent remarks. I didn't know how I would ever live down this episode. How was I going to be *the very best* when I could not remain on top of a small, scared Brahma calf? The ride of no more than a few seconds changed my world inside out. But by the grace and protection of the Almighty, I survived yet another day without shattered bones or visible wounds. I dusted off my clothes and picked up the hat that had fallen on the ground nearby.

As I walked with Dad, Mom and Pascal toward the house and a fresh cup of coffee, I had recovered enough to begin thinking about alternate potential endeavors. One thing for sure, I decided that the sport of bull riding should be left to others, and Durwood needn't worry about any forthcoming attempt by me to unseat him as the reigning family champion. That job was his for as long as he wanted it! I would seek out a more pain-free occupation.

I've often admired individuals who make their dreams come true by grit and self-determination, and as they journey through life, small roadblocks and detours seldom alter their goals. But I concluded, after much deliberation, that these people never experienced true pain as I did on that hot July afternoon when my rodeo career ended as quickly as it began!

Great occasions do not make heroes or cowards; they simply unveil them to the eyes of men.

—Bishop Westcott

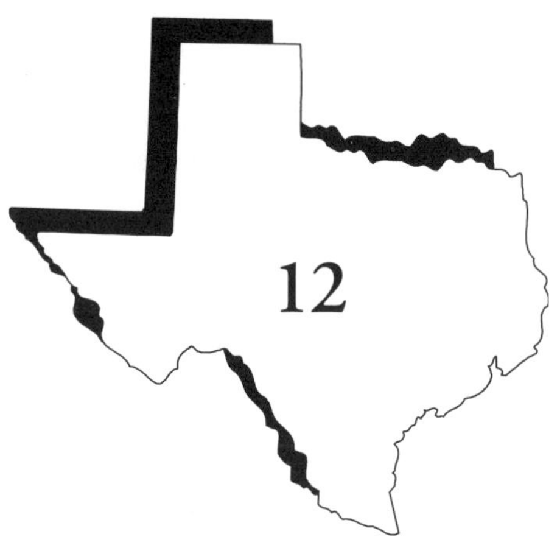

12

FIRST LOVES AND THE CREDIT GAME

AT THE BEGINNING OF THE THIRD GRADE I BEGAN to look at girls a little differently, but not enough to attract needless attention. I didn't want any of my buddies to think that I had gone soft on the issue of male chauvinism, so discretion became the watchword.

Ever since the first grade, I had always been fond of one of my classmates, Jody Dickerson, whom we called Jo-Boy. Once I asked how she came by that nickname. She said that her father thought her quite a tomboy, so he altered the term and substituted Jo for tom. All of this made perfectly good sense to me, because during our numerous visits, Jo-Boy and I passed a lot of time together by throwing rocks into the air. One of these stones—surely a small boulder—fell and landed on my forehead, caus-ing a small cut that appeared much worse than it turned

155

out, considering the substantial loss of blood and tears. I still carry a scar from that wound.

Jo-Boy was the youngest of three girls in her family. Her dad, Joe, originally owned the house and the forty-acre farm that my father bought and we lived on, so we had always known the folks. My parents spent many an evening at the domino table playing Texas Forty-Two with Joe and his wife, Lena.

Jo-Boy's sisters were Mabel Lois and Mary Lou. Mabel Lois was a lot older, at least by three years, but that didn't matter one bit. I was totally smitten with this Venus incarnate, accentuated by her big blue eyes and blonde hair. Regardless of the age difference, I began to play out my hand and seek the affection of this fair-haired beauty.

On the school bus each day I became a little braver and moved closer until finally I was able to sit directly by her. At first I felt a little uneasy and for the life of me I couldn't figure out what I was going to say if she ever spoke or struck up a conversation. Several times I overheard her friends laugh at my amateurish flirtation overtures and state, "Fred Barry must be sweet on you."

Mabel Lois had no comment on the subject one way or the other. She never complained about my constant, although silent, attention. I took this as a good sign—maybe a green light—so I continued the daily sortie on the bus and in the lunchroom. At some point, I threw caution to the wind, and determined that the possibility of romance far outweighed the probable ribbing by my buddies.

Before I go further, however, I digress. Dad always ran credit accounts at the local general stores and he had one with Preston Ainsworth. After the crops were sold or upon his return home from an out-of-town pipeline job, he would go to Preston and settle up. My dad was very wary of running up huge bills, and by paying all obligations promptly he guarded his credit rating wisely. At the age of eight, I didn't quite understand how the game worked. I sensed, however, that all you had to do to purchase something at Preston's store was to simply tell him to "charge it," but what was still unclear to me was that you had to fork over some currency at some point.

From my perspective, Mabel Lois and I became friendlier with each passing day, but I had to find a way to cement this new relationship. Although the method lay directly in front of me, circumstance would eventually control the outcome.

Every afternoon the bus driver stopped at Preston's. The kids who were lucky enough to have a coin or two got off, went into the store and purchased soft drinks, chewing gum or candy. Everyone welcomed these breaks before getting back on that dusty yellow bus for the final leg homeward. During one of these stopovers, I asked Mabel Lois if she would like a candy bar and a soda water—our expression for everything from Coke to Seven-Up.

"Sure," she answered, "but since I have no money, I'll have to pass."

I bragged, "Mabel Lois, that's okay. I'll buy it for you!"

Much to my understandable elation and then complete surprise, she smiled widely and immediately agreed. We stepped off the bus and into Preston's store side by side. I was so scared that I immediately began to question the reasoning behind all this effort. My mouth went dry and I could scarcely speak. I felt surely that my beating heart would wind up in my throat, causing a terminal case of asphyxiation. Even though I was probably suffering from a panic attack, I managed to carry on and put my best foot forward.

After carefully selecting our drinks and candy, we placed them onto the counter. By this time, things had settled to near normal. I looked up at Preston and boasted that I was paying for Mabel Lois' stuff.

He said, "Okay, sure, I understand." Preston winked at me the very moment when Mabel Lois wasn't looking. That embarrassed me a little, but matters quickly took a turn for the worse when the storekeeper tallied and announced the purchase at a whopping twenty cents.

I stood there like a dummy, after realizing that I was a nickel shy. The clock was ticking, so I had to think fast! Under extreme pressure, an inspiration revealed itself, coming to mind with the stroke of genius—more like a bolt of lightning, an epiphany of sorts.

"If I had only thought of this before!" I remarked to myself. "Why, this idea is nothing short of brilliance!" Without so much as batting an eye, I looked at the storekeeper and did exactly as my dad did every time he bought something. I said, "Since I'm a little low on cash, charge it."

During the next few seconds, I trembled at the possibility of hearing, "Fred Barry, you know I can't do that." My reputation was on the line, and I didn't know how many chances would be afforded me to make a spectacular impression on Mabel Lois. Preston, a little hesitant initially, finally looked under the counter and pulled out a worn, dusty book from which he tore a sales slip. He wrote down the items and threw the ticket into a cigar box. Later and *without* my knowledge, he entered the amount into a ledger under my dad's name.

My plan had worked! Mabel Lois and I took our purchases, got back on the bus and enjoyed our cold drinks and snacks. What a feeling of exhilaration I experienced! I felt as gallant as Stonewall Jackson must have after he had outflanked General Joe Hooker at Chancellorsville during the Civil War.

Well, a trend had been inaugurated. Each day thereafter, I acquired snacks for Mabel Lois, and it seemed that with every procurement, her admiration toward me increased. I thought, *Boy, what a deal! Now I understand what this thing courtship is about! All you have to do to get girls to like you is buy them soda water and candy.*

After two or three weeks, I decided to expand my base of operations. Mabel Lois had told Jo-Boy and Mary Lou that I had been footing the bill for goodies lately, and admittedly I felt a little guilty about leaving the two other sisters out of the circle, so I began to treat them to refreshments and snacks each day. Now I had three girl friends and I felt marvelous. This procedure continued for about three months without the slightest hint of trouble on the horizon. I had finally discovered, or so I believed, the secret of buying anything that one wanted by charging it.

One afternoon my mother said that Dad's job had played out; the pipeline was finished. He was coming home and would be here tomorrow when I got back from school. That was great news, because Dad had been gone for quite a while. Mom and I had really missed him.

The next day at school was unusually slow. I was eager to get home to see Dad, and when the bus finally

SALVE
BOOKS
GROCERIES
CHARGE IT!
Calvin Blassingame

stopped in front of my house, sure enough, he had arrived. What a joy! I ran inside, where he met me with open arms, a huge smile and a big bear hug. As usual, I expected a gift. He always brought me something, even if only a comic book. This time he showed up with a rubber tomahawk and a Choctaw Indian headdress, purchased in Oklahoma, a location that gave both items special significance and indisputable authenticity.

We sat around for a few minutes and talked about this and that. Everything was going well, until suddenly Dad spoke out, "Boy, you almost got me in trouble today!"

Naturally I didn't know what he meant, until he explained himself in greater detail. Earlier that day, he had gone to see Preston to pay the grocery bill in full, but when presented with the total, he was shocked and said to the storekeeper, "Preston, there's no way that I could owe you that much. Something's wrong. Surely you must have misfigured, because my total and yours don't add the same. Either that, or you're trying to swindle me!"

As you have already suspected, Preston produced the supporting documentation, and the two reviewed each sales slip very thoroughly. Dad knew right away which purchases were his, but for those that were left, he had no idea how they managed to get into his name. Preston thought for a second and explained, "Oh, those belong to Fred Barry. As of late, he's been buying soda water and candy for himself and the Dickerson girls on a pretty regular basis."

Now, before you start equating my questionable behavior to the failed savings-and-loan scandals of the 1980s and the Enron and WorldCom accounting schemes of 2002, let me first explain that the grand total of my expenditures came to $11.20. To my dad, however, that amount was unexpected and appeared to be outrageous—plus he had never given either me or Preston permission to charge anything to his account. But Dad soon cooled down and reconsidered. A true gentleman honors his obligations, even though part of them could be laid at the doorstep of an errant son who would probably claim that he didn't know any better. So he settled up the bill, got a receipt and came home to greet me.

As ordered, I sat down on the sofa—that always got my undivided attention. Although Dad had the stern *look*, smiling eyes shined through his expression. I noticed that immediately, so the consequences of whatever I had done seemed far less serious. He must have been torn at the thought of meting out punishment so close to our reunion, because he patiently began to explain the ins and outs of the credit industry. But when he started to harangue, I knew that I was in for an extremely long afternoon.

"Son, you are going to learn another valuable lesson today. It is one that comes at such a tender age, one that some people never master, no matter how long they might live, but this is one that you will never forget, if I have anything to do with it."

The pontificating seemed endless. Dad established that I had unmistakably learned the first part of the credit process, which was to say "charge it," but I must have been absent from class when they taught the second half of the course entitled *Pay for It*.

I failed to see either the necessity or the humor in all this verbiage, and admittedly, I was totally confused. Dad, however, was an excellent teacher and began to get through to me that until I was big enough to earn my own money, I should not spend his to buy anything for my girl friends. He ordered me to stop this business immediately and continued with the usual jargon about whipping you-know-what if he ever found out that I had a recurrence.

Much to my relief, he said I would not have to repay him. He would let me off for this one time only, but he recommended strongly that I always remember that *ignorance is no excuse under the law*.

I had successfully escaped the state of indentured servitude, thereby ensuring that the rank of bond-servant would never be added to my future resumes. But another major problem remained, one that would perhaps pose a more somber threat. Even though I now understood my dad's dictum—well, maybe not entirely—I didn't know how to stop such a popular practice, honed to precision and firing on all cylinders.

I asked Dad, "What am I to do tomorrow when we stop at Preston's store? How will I break the news to Jo-Boy, Mary Lou and Mabel Lois? What if they get furious? How can I ever face them again? If I do this, then I'm going to lose all three girl friends!"

"Son, you'll just have to pay for the goods yourself, but since you don't have any loose money lying around that I know of, you're going to have to be honest with them."

Now that's easier said than done. Remember that I'm only eight. The next day was one of the most miserable of my life, up to then anyway. I didn't know what to say to the girls, so I avoided them as best I could. That afternoon during the ride home, I tried to sit as far away as possible. In fact, I tried to hide, but that's not an easy thing to do when you're on a school bus that holds only fifty passengers. Sure enough, when we stopped at Preston's store, the moment of truth arrived! The girls soon spotted me, stopped by my seat, and inquired whether I was getting off to buy them soda water and candy.

I answered, "I can't."

"Why not?"

"I just can't."

"Does this mean you don't like us anymore?"

"No," I said. "I do still like you."

During that tense session, I brushed aside the lesson in honesty that my dad had recently bequeathed me. Once more, my common affliction, the problem of communication failure with the female gender, reared its ugly head! For the sake of me, I could not summon the courage to admit to the girls that I had been stupid for three months, so I kept quiet. Besides, they would never believe the real reason why I could no longer be their sugar daddy, a term that I often heard in a Hank Williams' song. And too, I had not yet acquired the knowledge that when dealing with the opposite sex, silence becomes one's most vile enemy! The girls, concluding naturally that I must be incensed or something, went back to their seats and started whispering amongst themselves, surely about yours truly and my misdeeds of the day. That credit fiasco promptly put my love life on hold. It took a couple of years to get over those first amorous adventures, but as far as credit is concerned, that took much longer.

When I reached the age of seventeen, Dad decided that it was time for me to take the first giant step toward manhood and fiscal responsibility. He walked with me into a Sears store in Beaumont, Texas and introduced me to the credit-sales manager. Cal Leatherwood reached for an application form and asked if I had previous credit background. Dad smiled and noted, "Oh, yes, he is very experienced in the field. Do you want references?"

When the credit manager nodded, Dad added, "I'm not really serious. This is a private joke!"

Leatherwood agreed to open the account in my name, with the proviso that Dad would cosign, which he did without hesitation. *That wasn't so bad*, I thought. Afterward, I selected a sewing machine for my soon-to-be bride, but I really didn't grasp what I had gotten myself into until about thirty days later when it came time to make that first easy payment. As I wrote the check, sealed it in an envelope and placed it in the mailbox, the faded statement of years past came back ever so clearly. "Son, you have to pay!"

Years later I met Cal Leatherwood again and in good humor blamed him for approving my first credit account. We both had a good laugh. But I never advised the Dickerson girls why I quit treating them, and they never asked a second time. Now and then, however, when thoughts return to those days of innocence, I'm sure that this crisis, which became one of the benchmarks of my life, never crossed their minds again.

Education is the ability to listen to almost anything without losing your temper or your self-confidence.

—Robert Frost

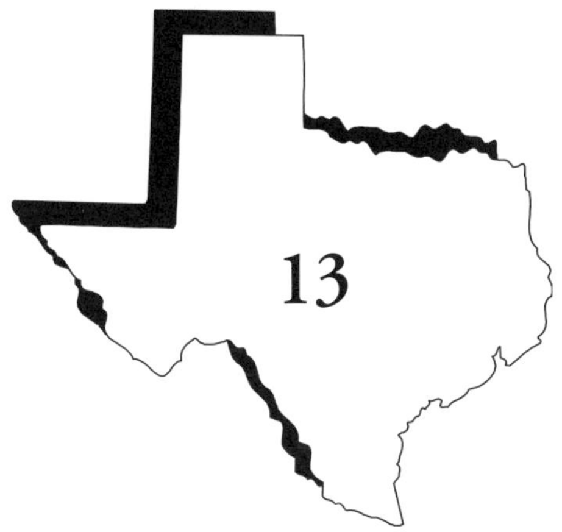

HUB CHRISTIE, PUPPIES, THE LAW AND FRIED RABBIT

UBERT "HUB" CHRISTIE WAS THE HALF-BROTHER of Altie Loggins, who became the third wife of my grandfather, Pony Wright. Dad had known Hub since childhood and often remarked—for good reason I might add—that he was three bricks short of a full load. In fact, Dad went a little further with this perceptiveness and emphasized that Hub was a little touched in the head and devoid of all common sense.

Once Dad mentioned that as they were walking home from some country-dance, Hub, for no reason, pulled a large knife and put it to my dad's throat, saying, "You know, Fred, I could kill you if I wanted."

When Dad told him in no uncertain terms to put away the blade, his longtime friend laughed, folded the weapon and slipped it in his pocket. Hub was just that way. No one ever knew when he was going off on one of those psychotic exploits, or what would trigger them, so my mom always cautioned me about having any direct contact with him whatsoever. However, when Hub moved into the Temple Loggins house, situated between ours and cousin Johnny "Tudor" Wright's, Mom underscored the warning, constantly advising me never to stop and converse with the new neighbor unless another adult was in my company. At first I did just that. But he always kept a bunch of dogs, and I do love dogs!

Hub had recently acquired a small female puppy that I considered extra special, and she followed me regularly during my walks on the way to play with Tudor. The dog, named Belle, and I became good friends, so I decided to ask Hub if I could have her. Frankly, I didn't understand why he needed another pooch, and besides, he wasn't feeding her properly. The animal's small ribs were plainly visible, and that, according to my standards, presented a pitiful and totally unacceptable situation.

Knowing that Mom's good cooking would soon put some meat on those bones, I began my quest for the puppy. How to accomplish that, however, was another matter. Mom forbade me to talk with Hub on a one-to-one basis, but the dog issue became paramount even in the face of those direct and irrefutable orders.

So I developed a plan. I began to purposely go by Hub's house when I knew that he was home. When I found him in the front yard, I stopped by and cautiously initiated casual conversation, all the while keeping a certain safe distance from this crazy man. Hub and I had a lot in common—we both liked dogs. But with each passing day, the puppy's condition seemed to worsen, so time became critical!

When I finally found enough courage to ask him about a possible swap, purchase or ownership transfer by simple donation, the answer was a resounding no. But after several weeks of constant badgering, he finally wavered and gave me the dog, which I immediately sprang on an unsuspecting mother who really didn't need another mouth to feed. Mom resisted at first, but she finally relented. And as I predicted earlier, Belle was fat and fit as a fiddle before too long. She became my good buddy and constant companion for about six months, until she disappeared without a trace.

In any event, my recent acquisition established a distant, although fragile friendship between Hub and me. Additionally, I always viewed the lifelong bachelor with considerable compassion because I suspected that he rarely cooked and ate enough to sustain his gaunt and slender frame.

CHINQUA WHERE?

One Saturday as I sat on the porch with my mom and dad, Hub got out of some stranger's car that stopped in front of our house. He seemed a little nervous. I didn't think much about his twitching at the time, because generally this was normal behavior. He grabbed a cane chair to sit in, reared back and threw his hat on the floor. Mom offered him the usual beverage, and he accepted graciously. Even though Hub's shaking hands barely held the coffee cup, nothing seemed out of the ordinary until the sheriff's car pulled up, and Nathan Tindall, who had known both my dad and Hub for years, emerged from the driver's seat. Sheriff Tindall had always been a personal hero of mine, and once to my extreme delight, even let me hold his pistol during an election rally.

I greatly admired the law profession. During our trips to San Augustine, I took every opportunity to hang around the courthouse grounds, where I caught glimpses of the sheriff and his deputies; the police chief and his deputies; the city marshal, who carried two pearl-handled six-shooters strapped to his legs in the fast-draw fashion; the constable; and the most revered of all—the Texas Ranger. In the presence of such great authority figures and all their firepower, I suppose it came natural for an impressionable youngster to stand in awe and feel extremely safe from all undesirables.

I also surmised that maybe that's why I never heard much about criminal activity on the contemporary local scene, especially shootings and killings. I did, however, find out later that San Augustine was one of the roughest and toughest towns in early Texas, gaining a lot of notoriety from its blood feuds, lawlessness and swift justice by well-attended public hangings on the courthouse square. All such affairs had ceased by the time I made my first trip to town, but I couldn't help but dwell constantly on the past and think about those reported shootouts that occurred in the hardware store and on the city streets.

Only once before had anyone in my immediate family claimed firsthand knowledge of a real desperado, and he came in the form of Jule Brown who passed by our house daily on his way to carry on clandestine operations. Mom said that the notorious bootlegger, who lived way back in the woods near Grapevine, kept the entire area supplied with moonshine whiskey, homebrew and other forms of hooch. Now Mom had no use for any part of the alcohol industry—manufacturing, distribution and selling or consumption. Recalling that Dad liked an occasional nip or two, she often used this topic as a platform from which to vehemently denounce and counsel me on the evils of drink.

So when Sheriff Tindall entered our front gate that Saturday morning, I was not duly alarmed. The lawman exchanged greetings, had some coffee, sat down and talked about the weather and such. Everyone thought this visit friendly enough until the sheriff remarked bluntly, "You know, Hub, you just shouldn't have cut him!"

My dad, Mom and I dropped our jaws at this revelation.

Tindall continued, "There's no reason to have done what you did, Hub."

Hub glared at him and responded with a string of profanity that would most assuredly wilt a patch of fully matured garlic.

"Nathan, I'm just sorry that I didn't kill the sorry son of a bitch for what he did to me. Do you know the son of a bitch pulled the wrong tooth? I'm telling you—he did! He deserved everything he got and then some." As you probably guessed already, Hub's favorite cuss words centered on that phrase *son of a bitch*.

The diatribe would not end here. Observably Hub felt the obligation to repeat every possible expletive known to modern man, so he extended the verbal onslaught by deploying language that I feel, in most cases, would embarrass the most accomplished of all reprobates. Finally, Sheriff Tindall heard enough and directed Hub to simmer down.

At long last silence prevailed, the contrast came into focus, the fuzzy reception cleared, and we were getting the full picture about how the hostility evolved. It seemed that earlier in the day, Hub hoisted a few too many, and then discovered that he had a terrible toothache. I couldn't understand how he could have possible felt anything, considering the extraordinary number of beers he admitted consuming.

Be that as it may, he drove to San Augustine where he demanded that the local dentist do something to relieve the miserable pain and suffering. He had to have some relief! But given Hub's advanced state of inebriation, Doctor Hicks couldn't pin down the exact molar that caused the immediate problem, so he asked the soused patient to make a positive identification. From a practical viewpoint, that request wasn't as simple as first suggested, because for years, Hub's great priority never revolved around the pursuit of beautiful, much less healthy teeth.

He could not have cared less about regularly scheduled maintenance visits, so by all rights, Hub should have been toothless long before this day ever arrived. Unfortunately, Dr. Hicks couldn't resist delivering a few verbal reprimands to a patient who seldom darkened his office door. This advice, however intentioned, did not bode well for the good doc, given the seriousness of the situation.

With all what-ifs, maybes and hindsight aside, Hub followed the dentist's command, grunted and aimed an unsteady finger toward the general area where the agony persisted. Somehow the communication blurred, and as luck would have it, Doctor Hicks extracted one of the better specimens, which posed no present threat or discomfort. The error spawned fierce retaliation! When Hub realized that the ache had not subsided, he lost his temper, cussed to the extreme, then pulled a knife and delivered several slashes to Dr. Hick's midsection and forearm. We learned later that the wounds were superficial, but at the time I remember thinking that this was a horrible thing for one human being to do to another.

After the sheriff finished his coffee, he thanked my mom, bade farewell to my family, turned to Hub and calmly said, "You do know, Hub, that I'm going to have to take you in."

"Sure," Hub responded, "you have to do your job. I understand that. Do what you have to do, and I won't give you any static in the meantime."

Neither seemed to be in a hurry, and there were no handcuffs. The two walked to the car together. Sheriff Tindall got in on his side, and Hub walked around front and sat down in the passenger's seat, just like they were going for a leisurely Sunday drive in the...I would have said country, had not they already been there.

"That is a strange sight," I stated. "Why, that's nothing like those rough-and-tumble arrest scenes in the gangster movies that I've seen playing at the theater in San Augustine."

Dad looked my way and told me to tighten up; I had a lot to learn yet. Regardless of the situation, I should wait to pass judgment. He reiterated something about justice and how everyone is assumed innocent until proven guilty.

"Oh well," I said, "as long as you know what it means, it sounds good to me."

Hub turned toward us briefly, smiled and waved one final time. Then the sheriff's car disappeared in a cloud of dust.

Dad shook his head in disbelief and remarked something about that "Crazy Hub, what will that crazy bastard do next?" Mom, however, offered a bit of sympathy when she said, "Poor old Hub, he's to be pitied."

Talk about passing judgment, huh?

Even though Hub had added another layer of tarnish to his shady reputation, I still considered him as a friend. *Anybody who loves dogs can't be all bad, I thought. After all, everyone gets upset every now and then—and in the interim, do something that they would love to take back later on.* So I chose to look on his better side.

Over the short term the dentist's injuries healed, the brief trial ended and Hub gained release after promising the magistrate that from now on, he would mend his ways and stick to the straight and narrow. My dad always said that Grandpa McKinley, a former county commissioner, personally spoke in Hub's defense and in fact swayed the jury to let him go without either a fine or additional jail time. Hub became a free man and returned home, but now with the benefit of in-depth reflection, even I looked upon him with greater skepticism.

After Dad purchased my horse gun, which is discussed in Chapter Fourteen, I tired quickly of bagging my limit of armadillos, so my sights were reset to target Chinquapin's more than ample rabbit population. I wasn't especially good at hunting cottontails, because I could never shoot them on the run. At the initial stage of the game, the species remained relatively safe. One day, however, to my absolute amazement, I dropped a huge buck from about twenty-five feet. Naturally, I felt that I should share the grand occasion with my parents.

Dad was home that summer working in the fields, and he just happened to be at the house when I arrived sporting the trophy slung across my shoulder. Over the course of the next few minutes, however, I found myself wishing that I had engaged in some other form of pastime. We had never eaten rabbit to the best of my knowledge, so I thought it strange to hear Dad say, "Myrtle, why don't I skin this critter, and you cook it for supper?"

"Rabbit!" I exclaimed. "We're going to eat rabbit?"

TASTES JUST LIKE CHICKEN!

"Son, we've eaten squirrels, and once we even ate a barbecued coon, so what's wrong with this rabbit? It's going to be clean, and I'll guarantee that when your mother's through with it, you won't be able to tell the difference between this and fried chicken."

"I'll be dog-dipped," I declared. "If it tastes like fried chicken, then I suppose it will be all right."

From out of left field Mom muttered, "Why don't we play a trick on Hub?"

Now that was strange indeed, especially coming from my mom, who usually didn't lean toward participating in practical jokes. Dad, on the other hand, always the rounder, picked up on the idea with great enthusiasm and stated, "Sure, we'll invite Hub to eat with us tonight. He probably needs a good meal anyway, and we'll fool him into thinking it's chicken."

When first hearing about these dining plans, I didn't know that Hub had a known history when it came to his eating habits, but Dad filled me in. It seems that Hub had bragged many times over the years that he would never eat a dammed old rabbit, no matter how hungry he got.

Dad looked at me and ordered, "Son, go down to Hub's and ask him to supper. Tell him that we're having fried chicken. I know that he won't turn that offer down."

"But, Dad, what if he won't come?"

"He will. Trust me, he will."

Now this put me in a very awkward situation! On one hand, I never told my dad no to anything, and on the other, I would be lying to Hub about that fried chicken. I remembered well how our good neighbor returned such favors.

The distance between our place and Hub's was probably no more than a quarter of a mile over the red-clay hill and down into a small clearing. From the top of the rise I had a plain view of his house. I distinctly remember praying that he wouldn't be at home when I got there. What if Hub found out that the *chicken* wasn't chicken after all, and that I was a party to this underhanded prank? I knew that he still had that knife and surely he might use it on me as he did on that dentist who pulled the wrong tooth.

All sorts of fears echoed through my mind, and as I came closer, sure enough, much to my regret, I saw Hub sitting in the front yard, perched on a straight-backed wooden chair, whittling on a piece of wood with that knife. I must have seemed unusually skittish myself when I approached and issued the supper request.

"Hub, Mom and Dad want you to eat supper with us."

"What are you having, Fred Barrow?" He always mispronounced my middle name.

"Chicken. Fried chicken, and I hear that's your favorite."

"Yeah, you heard right, boy," he said, and the two of us lit out immediately for our house.

When we arrived, Mother was busy frying chicken. Hub, Dad and I sat on the front porch passing time until Mom hollered that supper was ready and to come get it. The two men responded at the first call and promptly seated themselves at the dining room table. I wasn't in all that great a hurry and tarried for as long as I could. I sat down just in time to hear Dad tell Hub that he sure hoped he liked the chicken, but that it might be a little tough, though, since it was one of the older hens in the yard. Mom looked at Dad—and smiled.

As Hub tore into the first bite, I held my breath. I wondered just how we were going to get out of this thing alive. Furthermore, I knew that Hub had his knife with him, because I saw him put it inside his pants pocket. Reluctantly, I picked up a piece of the meat and tried it. I thought it tasted pretty good, though I would have never admitted it, even in the face of physical torture.

Hub kept himself busy with the chicken, mashed potatoes, biscuits and red-eye gravy, remarking just how good the main course was.

"Why, Myrtle, this chicken isn't tough at all."

What a relief, I thought. *He doesn't suspect a thing, and we're home free.*

When the last morsel was gone, Dad pushed away from the table, looked at his friend and dropped the bombshell. "Hub, how did you enjoy that fried rabbit?" The emphasis seemed to be on that now-dreaded word, *rabbit!*

I couldn't understand why Dad said what he did. Why did he expose our family to the wrath that would follow? The headlines of some paper, somewhere, the next day would read: *Family Slain In Dispute Over Fried Rabbit.* I fully expected to be the first to experience the sting of cold steel. Wasn't I the one who issued the fateful invitation?

Well, I have learned over the years that life is full of surprises. Hub leaned back in his chair, winked at me, and announced to the family that he was proud to have friends and neighbors like us. He added that in the future, if we ever had fried chicken again, and we extended him an offer to join us, he surely would accept it on a moment's notice.

To this day I don't believe that our old acquaintance ever thought that he really ate fried rabbit. By the way, we never played another trick on him either. In a feeble attempt to apply some rationale to that old saying that lightning never strikes twice, I was greatly relieved that

Dad never again wanted to push the limits of an unsteady character named Hub.

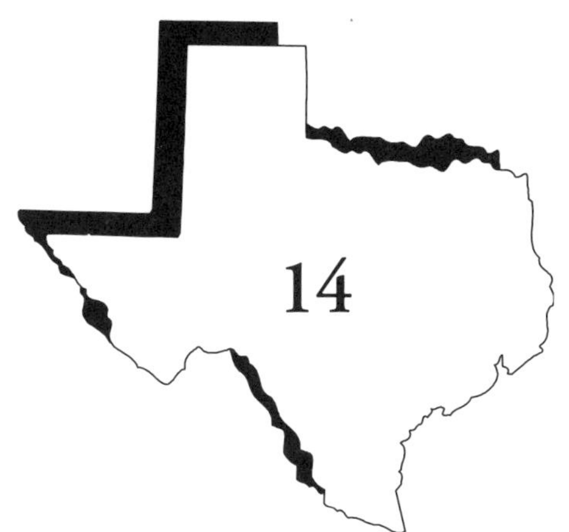

THE HORSE GUN

SINCE WE LIVED ON A FARM, I WAS OF THE OPINION that I should have a horse of my own, but this had never been the case. Dad owned a saddle horse once and promised me several times that as soon as I was old enough, he would buy one for me. I thought that perhaps he would give me his, but that was not to be either. Dad was a trader, and soon the saddle horse was gone in return for a gun, a dog and a little money to boot. I finally concluded that I would be the only boy in Chinquapin who would never have a mount of his own.

We owned various plough horses over the years, however, and I rode one in particular numerous times to visit my buddy, Lee Allen. Jim was a big Belgian, whose hooves seemed larger than my whole body. I felt a little awkward astride this big brute bareback and more than a little self-conscious about the whole topic, especially since

CHINQUA WHERE?

Lee Allen had a pony, saddle and all the trimmings. We must have looked like Mutt and Jeff riding our respective steeds down the red-dirt road toward my granddad Wright's country store.

When I came home from school one afternoon, Dad and Mom said that they had an important announcement and that it involved something that I always wanted. I thought immediately that maybe Mom was pregnant—I always hoped for a brother or sister—but Mom dashed those hopes immediately and instructed me to take another guess, this one on a more reasonable scale. After several misfires, Dad revealed that he had made some sort of pact with Random Hardy.

Random and his wife, Alma, lived up the road about four miles or so and had been close friends for years. Random was a farmer by necessity, but his true love lay in the art of financial enterprise. In other words, Random was one of those guys who would lend a poor laborer a dollar and allow him to pay him back at the rate of fifty cents per week over the period of a year. He was forever taking trades in place of those stiff repayment schedules, and that is how he became the proud owner of one of the prettiest buckskin mares that I ever saw. Without a doubt, she looked just like Buck, the horse that Matt Dillon rode later in the *Gunsmoke* television series.

GOTTA GET THAT BUCKSKIN!

It seemed that Random's mare was with foal, and as soon as the foal was born, it would belong to me. Of course, that was one of the most exciting days of my life. I even convinced myself that this was better news than any mention of a baby brother or sister.

The bus route took us by the Hardy farm each afternoon. For months I saw that mare getting larger and larger, and the anticipation of the blessed event caused the time to drag on incessantly. Frankly, I didn't realize that it took horses that long to gestate. Finally, one afternoon as the bus rounded the curve, I saw the mare with her new colt, a long-legged creature standing there and looking like it was hardly able to walk.

Why, he doesn't look like much! I thought, but as the days progressed, the colt got his legs, and I could see him running through the pasture. I had a name picked out already. He would be called Lightning.

All during this time I continually questioned Dad about when I was getting my horse. He explained patiently that colts had to be weaned, just like puppies. Now I understood that, but this was a far greater, more serious concern. We're talking about horses here, not puppies. Dad assured me that when he was old enough, we would get the animal and bring him home.

Again days turned into months, and I approached the panic stage. One morning I asked Dad about the horse once more. He directed me to sit down on the porch. He had something to tell me. When he spoke, I could not fathom what he said—something about things not working out the way that he planned and some other stuff that I didn't understand. He also added that horses eat quite a lot, and he decided that we wouldn't get the colt after all.

I was crushed! I had been patient, and this was just not right. How could a father go back on his word to his only son? Besides, every kid in school who had cared to listen knew about my horse. How could I go back and explain that it was all a misunderstanding? I felt that I would be the laughingstock of the entire school.

After a few crying nights—remember I was only nine years old—and sullen days, Dad said that he wanted to talk to me again. He explained how disappointed I must be, and that he might have a solution. He stated that we would go into town the next Saturday, and I could pick out a gun of my choice. I thought, *Fat chance! That's going to be just like my horse. I'll never get that gun either.*

I thought I was getting the raw end of the deal. Who would want a gun when he could have had a horse? But I kept my opinions to myself and tried to put the matter out of my mind. I didn't want to build up my hopes only to be let down once more, but on Saturday when we awoke, Dad instructed me to get ready. I asked, "Ready for what?"

He explained that this was the day when we were going to look for the gun, and only then did I realize that he really meant it. In the back of my mind I touched on the notion that maybe, just maybe, Dad was using this ruse to throw me off track. Perhaps I was going to get that horse after all, and he wanted to see just how mature I was. This could well be one of those tests in life that he always talked about.

Dad cranked up the truck, I got in, and we left for San Augustine. Since Mom chose not to go with us, I interpreted this as another potential tactic. Possibly she stayed home to ready the barn for the new arrival? Those hopes were dashed, however, when we passed Random's place and continued on toward San Augustine. I sat there, licking my wounds, feeling worse than ever, without uttering a word and battling back the tears.

When we arrived in town, Dad parked in front of the hardware store. I sat there until he advised me to get out and come in with him. The clerk greeted us and asked if he could be of any assistance. Dad responded, "Maybe you could show us some twenty-two rifles?"

I perked up immediately and for the first time put some stock in what Dad had mentioned earlier. He was really serious about buying a gun for me. Now wouldn't that be something, especially since all my friends, including Everett and Lee Allen, had owned theirs for years?

The clerk pulled out one of the most beautiful firearms that I had ever seen. It was a sleek Stevens single-shot .22, with a black barrel and shiny walnut stock. Dad examined it a while, then inquired about the price, which was fixed at about $19.95. Finally the bargain was struck, and I became the proud owner of that Stevens single-shot .22 rifle. I felt as big as any man, and the mental images of the buckskin colt faded quickly. Despite the previous setback, I now had a gun. To my way of thinking, this proved that my dad had confidence in me. Surely he believed that I wouldn't shoot myself during the first hunt.

When we arrived back at the house, Mom lectured Dad on what he had done. She told him that a nine-year-old had no business with anything like that, and she would make sure that I couldn't use it until I was old enough. I expressed my feelings. "Old enough! Old enough for what? My gosh, I'm nine years old. Besides, what's the use of having a gun unless you can hunt with it?"

After several minutes of pleading, I could tell that I had made a pretty good defense for my case. Mom finally let me go outside and shoot at some cans that Dad put atop several fence posts. After a few weeks she even allowed me to take the rifle by myself out in the woods, but I had to promise to be extra careful.

Dad also became quite involved in the safety issue. Of course, those instructions seemed unnecessary at the time. Besides, I had learned quickly how to use my Stevens .22, and I considered myself quite the professional.

The lesson that my parents tried to teach me didn't really mean anything until one afternoon when I learned about firearm safety the hard way. I had been in the woods and spotted a squirrel behind the limb of a great oak. After I cocked the hammer on the .22 and took a steady aim, the squirrel jumped into another tree, and off he went, never to be seen again. After an hour or two, I decided to head for home. I crossed the fence and came into the clearing at the top of the hill above our house. As I walked, I pointed the gun downward—but I forgot one important thing: the hammer was still cocked.

Suddenly it discharged! I flew into a state of panic when I felt a burning sensation in the small toe of my right foot. On that particular day, I was barefooted, a tradition that normally spanned March through October each year.

When the shot rang out, I hated to think about how to deal with a missing toe. I was already busy concocting stories to explain this latest catastrophe, but when I finally gathered enough strength to look down, there was no sight of blood. I thought, *Boy, what a relief.* But my legs continued to shake. I stood there for quite a while before fully regaining my composure.

Due to the location of the hole in the ground beside my foot, I decided that the bullet had missed the mark, but it came much too close for comfort. I was extremely lucky. Fate spared two things that day—my little toe and admitting to my parents that the great white hunter didn't yet know everything about handling his weapon. However, I never forgot this experience and never repeated that blunder.

As for the Stevens .22, I used that rifle for a long time, and scores of—well, maybe a few—armadillos, squirrels, rabbits and birds fell with its use. Over the years I have referred to it in conversations with my children as the "horse gun" and have fulfilled numerous requests to tell and retell the story. I never found out why I didn't get the colt, but I surmised that we honestly did not have the money for its upkeep. Though Dad never made any excuses, it must have killed his soul to break such a covenant.

Each day as I pass my gun cabinet, I think of that Stevens .22. I concluded long ago that if Dad had made good on his pledge and delivered as originally promised, Lightning would have ceased to exist as with all breathing, living things. But the rifle, a little faded with time but

still in good shape, remains as one of my fondest posses-
sions and continues to flood my memories of days long
past when a boy received a gift from his father that erased
the piercing disappointment associated with a buckskin
colt.

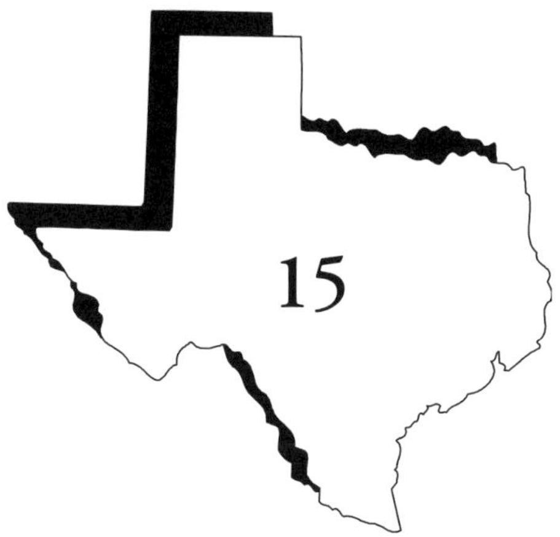

15

NICK AND THE JUNKYARD FORD

LATE IN 1951, DAD HIRED ON WITH A PIPELINE CON-cern in Kansas for a job that lasted several months. During the prolonged absence, he left Mom and me in charge of at least one milk cow, about a dozen chickens, a hog and an ornery mule whom we called Nick. From all recollections, Nick was much taller than my dad, who was about six feet. Dad held the large, black creature in high esteem and commented numerous times that he was one of the best working mules that he ever owned. He was relatively gentle, as mules go, and willingly shared the pasture with the other farm animals.

However, Nick had one serious flaw. As a world-class jumper, he failed to understand the true significance of fences and viewed them as small nuisances that kept

DON'T FENCE ME IN!

him from the outside world and greater adventures. With every escape, the usual search commenced, and after several minutes, I would find him grazing in the pasture of some adjoining neighbor.

Although Nick liked a certain amount of freedom, he never strayed so far that he couldn't be found in the short term. In some ways, he reminded me of the kid who always alerted his parents of the planned destination before he ran away from home. I am not a psychologist, but to me, such behavior demonstrates an inherent desire for security. Mom described this tendency in more colorful language when she said, "He was a whole lot like some people: they not only want their cake, they want to eat it too."

That's the way Nick seemed to carry on, and after a while, I came to know his favorite hangouts. Each time turned out the same. When I located him, he never ran or balked when I placed the rope halter around his huge head. He calmly followed my lead toward home, where he would remain for a few days, only to repeat the process. I suppose that Nick always knew that someone would come looking for him.

One afternoon, I went with Mom to tend the chores. As we walked across the pasture toward the barn, both of us realized that Nick had gone AWOL. While milking the cow, feeding the chickens and slopping the hog,

Mom expressed the usual displeasure about the recent breakout. She remarked that we had better things to do than go to Heaven knows where, looking for Nick, who seemed to be getting habitually worse as time wore on.

"I don't know why your dad just doesn't get rid of that old mule," she said. "He's actually more trouble than he's worth!"

Although it was extremely hot that evening, I put in the required effort and completed the customary rounds. After a couple of hours, however, I called off the search with Nick still on the loose. At first, Mom worried that I came home without my charge, but she said that he would surely turn up sooner or later.

The following morning we were greeted by a knock on the front door. To our surprise, it was Johnny Neal Wagstaff, a distant cousin, nearby neighbor and older brother of another of my best friends, Larry. In the beginning Johnny Neal stood there, looking down at the floor, and only after several prompts by Mom did he summon the nerve to say anything. He finally stated that his dad had sent him on a mission.

It is true that the Wagstaffs were relatives, but we always viewed them as the black sheep of the family. I always considered them to be Chinquapin's version of Ma and Pa Kettle with all those kids, dogs and cats running loose and out of control. In retrospect, it is entirely plausible that most folks in San Augustine proper probably viewed *all* the residents of Chinquapin, including the McKinley household, in the same light. Mom never let me visit Larry, because she thought that I might return with some fearful disease of sorts caused by unwashed dishes and a house that had never been thoroughly cleaned. Larry's mother, Pauline, never measured up to Mom's high expectations about how a house should be kept.

With some reluctance, Johnny Neal explained that Nick had visited their place on his most current outing and initiated contact with one of their prize calves. Somehow Nick turned into a killer mule and stomped the poor animal to death. We thought this horrible, but as my mom began to question Johnny Neal about the incident, the facts became a little clouded. Mom always seemed to know how to get at the truth. Of course, she wanted to know when and how all this happened.

Johnny Neal responded that only yesterday they saw Nick come up the road, jump into their pasture and promptly kill the calf. It seemed that the entire Wagstaff family witnessed the ghastly occurrence, and no matter how hard they tried, no one could scare the mule away. It seems that old Nick must have been in some sort of trance.

"Maybe he's afflicted with that Dr. Jekyll and Mr. Hyde thing," I offered.

No one commented on my shrewd observation, so Johnny Neal continued with the gruesome details. He said that they at last captured Nick and that he was being held inside their barn until we came and retrieved him. But there was a hitch! Johnny Neal indicated that his dad placed a value of twenty-five dollars on the lost calf and that we would have to pay that amount.

Mom took a deep breath and exhaled loudly. Her facial expression changed within a blink of an eye. With flared nostrils and a menacing scowl, she put her hands on her hips, and said, "Now wait just a doggoned minute!"

I had never seen Mom so upset. She viewed this message as a ransom demand, a shakedown and an extortion plot, all rolled into one. Up until that very moment, she never particularly cared for Nick, but now we were talking about something entirely different; this was a new ball game. After all, the mule was part of the family, and everybody knows that kin stick together. She informed Johnny Neal that we would be along later to talk to his dad and get this matter straightened out once and for all.

As with most proud people, Mom is one of those individuals who would fight to the death on principle. If she believed that Nick had done the terrible deed, then she would have found the twenty-five dollars somehow and paid for the mule's purported capital offense. In her opinion, however, it was much too early to begin discussing reparations and damage awards. Besides, she had not yet begun the investigation.

After Johnny Neal left, both of us talked about Nick in great admiration and how he could not possibly be the killer that had been described. In fact, we believed that Nick had been framed for a crime that he did not commit. Mom looked at me and said, "Come on, let's get your Grandpa McKinley! We're going over to those Wagstaffs and get to the bottom of this."

She stalked out of the house toward the Ford. Now this was not just any ordinary Ford. Dad had bought this jewel from Tindall's Junkyard a couple of years before. I knew this because when he brought it home for the first time, both front doors showed the printed words "Tindall's Junkyard." We scraped off the letters and tried to make it a little more presentable by covering up the residue with some matching black paint. That didn't help much, but at least we tried. Regardless of appearance, though, this was one of the first cars that we ever owned, so I suppose one could say that it did elevate our family's social standing within the community, if only a tad.

Much to our chagrin, however, the Ford did not operate any better than it looked, because it frequently failed to respond when Dad turned the key to the ignition. In reality, it was downright unreliable, no question about that. I never knew whether the problem originated with a weak battery, bad generator or what, but in order to start the motor in most instances, we had to push the car and then throw the manual transmission into gear. Sometimes it worked; other times not. Strong backs, combined with a touch of patience and ingenuity, were the order of the day. Consequently, Dad always tried to park on an incline, which would make the difficult process far easier the next time around. Of course, all of this pushing nonsense caused extreme embarrassment to me, especially in front of my friends, and frankly, I never understood why he didn't bite the bullet, go out and buy a more suitable vehicle.

Anyway, back to the saga of Nick. When Mom and I passed the Ford and started down the road toward my grandparents' house, she paused and said, "Let's take the car." I stopped in my tracks, paused briefly, swallowed hard and thought, *What did she just say?* Her comment came out of left field, and it took me by complete surprise! To the best of my knowledge, Mom had driven only once before and that was under extreme duress. She never found comfort behind the wheel, so that duty always fell to Dad. Now she wanted to take the car—will wonders never cease?

I viewed the announcement with great perplexity, but my arguments against her idea fell on deaf ears. I could not persuade Mom to change her mind. She was hell-bent on getting to the Wagstaffs' as soon as humanly possible, so I followed orders and assumed my usual position as the assistant propulsion engineer near the back bumper, all the while praying that the engine would falter and cause us to seek alternate means of transportation. I didn't trust Mom's driving ability for one instant.

After several attempts, however, the motor started somehow or another, much to my bewilderment and fear. I crawled in the passenger seat, shut the door and off we went down the dusty road amidst the grinding sounds and all the associated problems surrounding a person trying to drive with a stick shift on the floor for the second time in her life.

Finally we arrived safely at the bottom of the hill below my grandparents' house. A narrow dirt road, deeply rutted, led off the main thoroughfare up a steep embankment. Considering the rocky start, we negotiated the hill with relative ease and found Grandpa McKinley on the front porch, sitting in his favorite rocking chair and whittling on a piece of wood.

Mom quickly explained Nick's quandary and asked if he would go with us to talk to the Wagstaffs. He answered in the affirmative, and we all went to the car. Before opening the door, however, I remembered that my grandfather didn't drive either. Small beads of sweat appeared on my forehead when Mom once again took the helm! I looked down the hill toward the main road, knowing that three possibilities existed—we could go the left, which was the correct way; we could go to the right; or we could go straight ahead and wind up amongst the unknowns at the bottom. Trees, vines and tall weeds blocked the vision of certain dangers that lay below. I do not know to this day what Mom was thinking about. I suppose that she was too caught up in anger toward the Wagstaffs, and her adrenaline must have outweighed all common sense.

Once again, the car started miraculously, and we started the descent. This was a good sign—but right away, things went awry. Instead of slowing down for the upcoming left-hand turn, it seemed that we were picking up speed. Grandpa hollered at Mom, "My God, Myrtle! Slow this thing down or we'll go over the side!"

Mom responded in time and with trembling voice, frantically stating something about how the brakes weren't working. I thought, *That's great! The son of a gun won't start half the time, and now the brakes are bad. What's next?*

We continued onward at breakneck speed. I heard the repeated sounds of the brake pedal slam against the floorboard as Mom tried in vain to slow the vehicle, but all attempts failed. Just when we were braced for the expected unavoidable crash, somehow Mom steered to the left. We turned the corner on two wheels, and fate brought us through the incident unscathed.

A few yards up the road, the car lost its momentum. When we finally stopped, Mom's left foot still held the pedal to the floorboard. She seemed paralyzed. Only then did pure terror hit me when my grandfather remarked, "Lord, Myrtle, you have your foot on the clutch! No wonder you couldn't slow down." After a few minutes just sitting there and collecting ourselves, we became amused at the failed "brakes." Then we recalled our reason for being there in the first place and continued toward the Wagstaff farm.

When we arrived, Johnny Wagstaff, Sr. met us at the front gate and greeted us in a neighborly fashion. Mom reciprocated but immediately began the inquiry into the allegations against Nick. Johnny recited the story just as Johnny Neal had earlier that morning, but somewhere during the narration, Mom began to harbor serious doubts about what really happened. She submitted rapid-fire questions, and I'm sure at that point, Johnny questioned his own motives and wondered why he stirred up such a hornet's nest. He would have had better luck with the devil himself.

Mom was not going to just take his word. The elder Wagstaff would have to do better than that, so she demanded to see the body of that slain calf. Somehow I supposed that Mom would be able to detect hoof marks and either prove or disprove the cause of death. Remember, I said that she had a way of getting to the facts of a case, however difficult.

Johnny told Mom that the calf's corpse had been taken up the road and discarded. Actually, he said, "Myrtle, we tuk that pore ole dogie up yonder a piece and throw'd it in a trash heap."

Complying with Mom's demand to view the remains, he sent Johnny Neal along as a guide. To make a long story short, a close inspection confirmed that the calf that we were expected to believe had been killed by Nick the day before had actually been dead for a lot longer than that.

Mom promptly went back to his house and called Johnny a coward for sending his oldest son to do his dirty work and a liar, emphasizing that he simply wanted to use a poor dead calf to weasel twenty-five dollars from us. With the entire Wagstaff clan looking on, she continued to give our distant cousin a good tongue-lashing.

"Johnny," Mom persisted, "you should be ashamed of yourself! How could you stoop so low and try to take advantage of us knowing that Fred is away?" Sarcastically, she added, "This must be one of your proudest achievements."

Mom prolonged the bombardment, and Johnny received no respite during this fierce, one-sided exchange. Momentarily my thoughts drifted to the Alamo and how the embattled Texian force, gravely outnumbered and outgunned, must have felt when they heard the song *Degüello*—the "fire and death call," roughly translated as calling for total annihilation or giving no quarter—hours before Santa Anna issued the final order of attack. Of course, I felt no sympathy toward Johnny, but I had no idea what his response would be, nor the form it might take.

I winced, thinking that worse was yet to come, but surprisingly, Johnny said and did nothing. I guess that he was too shocked to react. Grandpa remained silent also, concluding rightly that Mom had everything under complete control. She took advantage of the temporary lull, stormed to the barn and rescued Nick. No one dared say anything, much less make an attempt to block her passage. I guess that Johnny figured the jig was up, because he never again mentioned the twenty-five dollars.

Mom mumbled something like, "That will certainly teach him a thing or two about dealing with us in the future. Johnny Wagstaff didn't know what he was getting himself into when he opened that can of worms." I thought Mom's description a little mild; it was more like blowing off the lid with a stick of dynamite and unleashing the horrid contents of Pandora's Box.

Grandpa walked back to our house with the freed mule in tow, and with the protection of Providence, Mom and I also made the return trip unharmed. At least she had learned the difference between a clutch and a brake.

Mom felt obligated to take Grandpa home when he was ready to leave. When he heard this offer, though, the old man shook his head and responded, "Now don't take this the wrong way Myrtle, but if it's just the same to you, I'd feel much safer by walking." I couldn't blame him—the decision made perfectly good sense to me.

Grandpa and I placed Nick in a small enclosure by the barn, and for some reason, we closed the gate. "A lot of good that will do," I scoffed.

As we turned to step away, neither of us could help glancing back to make sure that Nick remained put. But for the time being, he seemed to be content, and I swear that he appeared happy to be back on familiar turf. Within a few days, however, he continued his escaping ways, but we never again heard of him heading toward the Wagstaff farm.

I had always heard that old dogs weren't capable of learning new tricks. But when comparing dogs with mules, however, I wondered whether the same rationale applied. I also knew that mules were known for their stub-bornness, a trait that I witnessed almost daily. So after con-siderable youthful thought, I came to two conclusions: by staying clear of the Wagstaffs', Nick did learn some-thing new, but he was just too stubborn to allow us to think that he had completely changed his rambling ways.

All animals but men know that the principal business of life is to enjoy it—and they do enjoy it as much as man and other circumstances will allow it.

—Samuel Butler

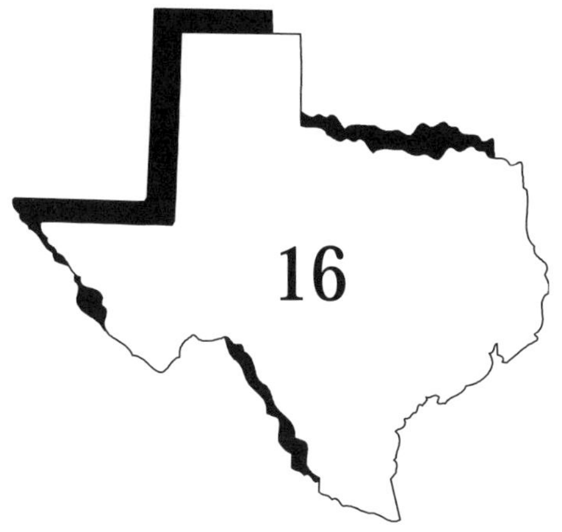

16

THE YOUNG ROCKY

URING SCHOOL RECREATION PERIODS OR RE-cesses, as we called them, there was not much to do other than participate in softball games, shoot marbles, ride swings, whittle with one's favorite knife or fool around on the slides and seesaws. So I assume that it came naturally for the boys to become involved in the sport of boxing. We referred to this ancient art form by using a much simpler term—fighting. Various factors brought on these minor fracases: comments from one or the other about some nonsensical issue, understood only by the male gender, or jealousy over the imagined over-tures of some young lass on campus. From the first day at school, I liked to engage in pugilism. Although I never considered myself a bully, I never ran from a good scuffle either.

CHINQUA WHERE?

Several cousins attended Chinquapin school, a home to ever-changing friendships and alliances. Each could therefore be a soul buddy one minute and a strong adversary the next. I fought many a scrap with Larry Wagstaff, who countered with open fingernails that left scratches for days on end. Although it appeared that I came out second best during these skirmishes, I rarely stopped until Larry fled the battle scene, leaving me to carry the day.

Now before I go any further, and you label this as outright barbarism, remember that we were small kids who were incapable of inflicting mortal wounds upon one another. Most fights ended with nothing more than a bloodied nose or swollen lip, and maybe a few tears. Additionally, we never began a fight with the intention of really hurting someone or with the notion that we would eventually pull a knife and inflict bodily harm. We viewed fighting as nothing more than an innocent pastime. Most teachers, however, did not interpret the sport in the same context because many a youngster who indulged in such conduct felt the sharp pains of correction on his backside.

One of my cousins, James Loggins, had severed an index finger just above the knuckle years before, and even though the doctor reattached the appendage, two flaws remained. Because the area above the joint never grew at the rate of the original below, James could never bend the repaired member enough to make a fist. Consequently, he literally fought with one arm behind his back. Many times, the two of us battled to a standstill, he with one good fist and me with two. No matter how hard I tried to overcome him, James, who never considered the handicap as weakness, matched me blow for blow. Afterwards, I always wondered how it would have turned out if he had two good fists. Deep down, I knew that he would have been the eventual victor.

I also swapped punches with two other cousins, Harold and Leon Loggins. Most of these conflicts ended in a draw, as did those with another friend, Lee Allen Dickerson. When these flare-ups were over, we soon forgot about them completely and with rekindled relationships, we roamed shoulder to shoulder over the school campus like nothing had ever happened.

There was one exception to the rule. To a man, all the boys on that rural campus hated Carlo de Carlo, a black-haired husky kid, who arrived in our school when I was in the second grade. Carlo quickly became the aberration who reveled in terrorizing the girls and small boys. Why, he even held the bluff over me.

One day, Carlo was up to his usual antics and had one of our school chums on the ground beating the living daylights out of him. Everyone stood around in a circle watching the terrible event, but no one made a move to intercede. Suddenly my blood pressure rose to critical levels and something came over me.

I had visited my cousin Pete in San Augustine the previous Saturday, and the two of us completed one of our customary all-day excursions to the theater, owned by Will and Atheniar Wade. We drank Cokes and munched on popcorn and candy while being treated to a double-feature movie flanked by numerous cartoons, two serial installments, previews of upcoming attractions, and the Movie Tone News. We were almost blind when we emerged from the show and walked into the bright sunshine.

One of these movies starred some western hero. But the subject of the other centered on a young prizefighter who lost many early bouts only to become world champion after his trainer taught him to fight close in and use quick short jabs to the body of his opponent.

Now on that school morning, I was witnessing Carlo de Carlo in all his glory doing what he did best. I knew that I had to do something! Remembering the fight scene from the previous Saturday, I abandoned all fear and jumped into the fray. Carlo pulled away from the other kid and stared me square in the eyes. With flared nostrils, he remarked that he was going to beat the tar out of me. Actually, he used a four-letter word, but I won't repeat that one here. My classmates must have thought that I had lost my ever-loving mind.

Carlo outweighed me by quite a bit and he held that terrible reputation as a brawler. There I stood, a small kid with no chance at all. My buddies must have surmised that I would not live past the morrow.

One girl in the crowd screamed, "Fred Barry, he's going to kill you!" After uttering that prophecy of doom, Jo-Boy Dickerson turned and ran toward the schoolhouse, yelling that she was going to get Mrs. Collins. I looked at Carlo and my blood boiled.

I suppose that individual genes, chromosomes and genetic makeup govern a person's behavioral patterns and how one reacts to specific encounters, but thoughts about such powerful scientific terms never came to my mind at that particular time. Later in life, I heard that the Irish and Scots, known for their terrible tempers, became involved in many needless battles throughout the ages. I even read where some distinguished writers blamed the South's loss during the Civil War on its Celtic leaders and soldiers who comprised the majority of the rebel armies. Drawing from this thesis, the authors wrote that the Celts were too hot-tempered and impatient to make logical battlefield decisions; the Southerners, therefore, charged many a Federal position of strength when they should have adopted more defensive postures.

I attacked Carlo de Carlo that morning with reckless abandon. I felt rage at the fact that he seemed always to hold the upper hand. I was tired of everyone giving in, letting him have his way continuously. I knew that he would never leave my classmates or me alone unless someone finally took up the gauntlet.

To say the least, Carlo seemed confused! I came fast, landing body blows to his stomach region. I knew also that if he ever hit me with one of his famous rights, it would be over in a heartbeat. So I continued with the inside strategy. Carlo backed up, and I fought on with the fury of my Celt ancestry.

"Leave us alone, you big bully!" I shouted.

After hearing this rendition of the Rebel Yell, my classmates screamed with delight and encouraged me onward. By this time, I felt great! I knew that I was winning and that Carlo appeared to be running out of steam. More than anything, Carlo was probably shocked that someone finally took the offensive to end his reign of terror. He didn't know how to check such a move.

About that time, Mrs. Collins arrived, quickly putting an end to the sparring match. She scolded us and pointed to the evils of fighting on the school campus. I didn't mind those verbal reprimands, but I dreaded what would surely follow. Had my time finally come? Would my noble efforts result in Pauline Collins' application of those long-evaded licks of corporeal punishment to my rear end? But again, maybe not! She looked downward in my direction and winked. That was a good omen.

Before Mrs. Collins turned and walked away, she smiled and decreed, "You boys quit that fighting! As for the rest of you, go back to playing. Recess will be over in about five minutes."

I was spared! During those happiest five minutes of the day, my buddies gathered around and congratulated me on my accomplishment. They recognized me as the one who finally brought Carlo's supremacy to an end— well, maybe not to an end, but at least to a temporary suspension. I turned toward Jo-Boy and asked why she summoned Mrs. Collins to stop the fight. In spite of my small size, the momentum had shifted, and I wanted to finish it once and for all. I wanted him to experience what he had been dishing out, but more than anything, I wanted to see him cry!

Jo-Boy shrugged her shoulders and replied, "I thought that he would hurt you. That's why."

That comment brought more self-adoration. Not only had I protected my classmates from certain future danger, I seemed to have garnered the attention of one of my favorite girl friends. Now I knew how the knights of old felt after winning one of those jousting tournaments.

My fighting success, however, was short-lived. No, the highly anticipated rematch with Carlo never occurred. Carlo came to his senses not long after that, and I don't remember him ever attempting to reestablish his bully label. Now I don't mean to imply that he became a saint or anything like that, but at least he became more tolerable.

No, my threat never originated from Carlo. It came from an unexpected source! James Loggins had a younger brother named Lue Dean who was a couple of grades behind me and of course much smaller. Somehow I must have upset him with some ruthless comment or action, but for the sake of me, I can't remember the actual event, whether real or imagined. Anyway, Lue Dean must have relayed the problem to James—and James must have passed it on to his older sister, Patsy.

Patsy Loggins was, at that particular time, a tall skinny kid, much larger than I was, but I don't remember anything more, except that she too was a distant cousin. One day after finishing a drink of water at the outside fountain, I felt a tap on my shoulder. I turned only to be greeted by the furious wrath of a female whom I finally recognized as Patsy. She met me with strong swift punches to the face and about the body; the brutal attack seemed to last for hours.

WANT MORE?

Shortly, I lay on the ground, tattered and embarrassed by the fact that a girl had beaten me to a pulp. In total humiliation, I looked up and posed that insightful question, "What did I ever do to you?"

Patsy replied, "Oh, nothing. It's not what you did to me—it's what you did to Lue Dean. Quit it. I mean it! Stop picking on my little brother."

During the next few days, my so-called buddies ribbed me about this affair. Time and time again, they reminded me that I could hold my own with Carlo, but I was no match for Patsy. Learning from my mistakes, I attempted, with little success, to stay clear of Lue Dean after that. Even though the little fellow annoyed me with constant references as to how his protector treated all opposition, I walked away without a word. I did not seek to challenge that old adage that lightning never strikes the same place twice. But in reality, I wanted no more— could stand no more—surprise visits from Patsy Loggins!

Shortly, this latest trauma died down, and it was overlooked by most. But I will never forget that day when Patsy Loggins administered one of the worst beatings—more like a complete and total ass-whuppin'— that I ever took on the grounds of the school at Chinquapin.

17

A LOT OF BULL

URING ONE OF MY DAD'S MANY TRIPS TO THE San Augustine cattle auction, he bought a young Brahma bull, about three-quarters grown, with the potential of becoming an excellent breeder. He already had a good set of horns and a big hump on his back, but his color, a distinctive blue cast, represented the defining highlight. At first we thought about calling him Blue, but the name Joe won out somehow or the other.

At first, Joe displayed a pleasing personality, but as he got older, he began to exhibit the trait for which Brahma bulls are known the world over—outright meanness. Because of his unsettled temperament and erratic mood swings, I respected his size and demeanor and gave him an extra-wide berth while walking across the pasture toward Everett's house.

Everett's dad, Truitt Henley, owned the farm that connected to ours. Truitt raised a lot of goats, but he also had a small, stocky Hereford bull who guarded his territory in much the same manner that Joe did. The two bovine neighbors met often and tried to settle their differences of opinion over who was really the king bull of the adjoining pint-sized fiefdoms. Boundary issues and macho attitudes were at stake.

Unfortunately neither recognized the obstacle of the fence that divided our properties, no matter that it was made of barbed wire, one of the most dangerous fabrics known to man and beast alike. Although there was never a clear winner, most brawls ended with both combatants receiving serious cuts that required immediate attention, otherwise infections would spread and those deadly hookworms would soon develop. The fencing also suffered dire consequences, being torn down in large sections, and it continually had to be replaced.

After several such bouts, Truitt came to our place and helped Dad pen up Joe, then drive him into one of the barn stalls to be patched up. Now the big fellow did not care for close quarters, much less the medical attention. The thought of pushing him into a corner and having him come out in reckless abandon, mad as all hell, scared the heck out of me.

Each time turned out the same. Everett and I climbed onto the barn roof and got ready for the customary spectacle. After assisting Dad in ministering to Joe's health-care needs, Truitt ran out of the barn and moved quickly over the top board of the corral fence, safely out of harm's way. Then Dad opened the stall gate, ran into the clear and followed Truitt's lead, with Joe bringing up the rear—snorting and bellowing what must have been obscenities understood only by bulls. After a while, the anger toned down considerably. When it appeared that Joe no longer posed a physical threat, Dad let him out of the corral, and we awaited the next duel between the feuding bulls that would most assuredly produce more exciting amusement.

Financial necessity dictated that my dad act out the role of a shade-tree veterinarian. One summer afternoon, he announced that we needed to give Joe a vaccination of some sort, and we had to prepare the patient to receive the remedy. I dreaded that part, having to go into the pasture and force Joe to do something that went against his very nature, or grain as we called it.

But this day, I was pleasantly surprised. The bull first responded with kindness. He then followed my dad's bidding and headed toward the barn and the enclosure, but when he arrived near the entrance, things immediately changed for the worse. When we began nudging him toward the gate, Joe stopped, turned and placed his head in a downward position.

As Dad had always explained, that stance meant that a bull was about to take big-time, serious offensive action. When Dad saw Joe begin to paw at the dirt, he screamed for me to get back. No sooner had I heard that command, the vision of what happened then came in slow motion, an idea that I had previously poked fun at.

Joe started to charge! At first he looked toward Dad, then in my direction. I guess that he considered a skinny, barefoot eight-year-old kid the better choice and the easier target because he came straight at me. Later in life I read and heard about near-death experiences, and when people say that life flashes before you during those terrifying moments, that's no bull—no pun intended. I saw the big monster coming and I knew that if I didn't move quickly out of his way, it would mean a certain and cruel death either by being gored mercilessly or trampled beyond recognition. Joe outweighed me by several hundred pounds, but as he neared, I stood there, frozen to the ground, unable to move. My heart nearly pounded out of my chest.

That was the first time that I experienced true, raw fear. I heard the hooves strike the ground as the brute rushed forward with savage force. Then from the corner

FEET, DON'T FAIL ME NOW!

of my left eye, I saw a form run between the would-be assailant and me. Someone waved frantically, shouting for the bull's attention. In an instant, Joe turned and ran into the open pasture, leaving me both breathless and trembling. Immediately afterward, I felt my dad grab me and ask if I was okay. Still in a semi-state of shock, I looked down and realized that I was not injured, only shaken. When I finally gained my composure, I saw my dad fold his pocketknife and slip it into his pocket.

"I really don't know what good that small blade would have been, but it was all that I had," he said.

No, it was not the knife that scared Joe into making the sudden turn that left me in one piece. My father came between us, thereby risking his own life in the process. Every Brahma bull that I've seen since brings back memories of that near catastrophe, and I suppose that Joe was the main reason why I never cared to watch rodeo clowns take such chances under similar circumstances. Talk about playing with fire!

I also learned another valuable lesson on that occasion. Throughout life we often hear people say, "I would have done this, or that."

That comment reminds me of the tale about two good ol' West Texas boys who were out one night hooting it up, drinking a few Lone Stars and generally having a good time. When the local watering hole closed, neither realized that a county sheriff patiently sat nearby in his patrol car, waiting on the next unfortunate victim to pass his way.

The two cowboys made their way to an old truck and started back to the ranch. Not wanting to bring undue attention to their current condition, the driver exercised extreme caution, or so he thought. He was puzzled at seeing flashing lights in the rear-view mirror. Sure enough, the sheriff motioned for him to pull over to the side of the road. The lawman got out and walked to the driver's side of the vehicle where he announced that the posted speed limit had been exceeded by some twenty miles per hour.

The driver disputed the accusation and claimed that this was just not so. "Surely the radar gun was wrong," he argued. But after a few minutes, the realization finally set in that he pursued a lost cause. So he accepted the ticket and asked if he could leave. Permission, however, was not granted. At that point, the sheriff walked to the other side of the truck, stopped and directed that the second occupant roll down his window. With that, he reached in, seized the passenger and slapped him a few times. As you might expect, this action prompted a barrage of questions as to the reason for such brutality.

"Hey! I was sitting here quietly, minding my own business. I did nothing to deserve such treatment, so why did you hit me?"

"When I get back in my car," the sheriff answered, "and you guys proceed up the road a piece, I know that the conversation would turn to whether you were actually speeding or not. I also know that you would have said to your buddy over there behind the wheel, 'If I had been driving, I would have told that son of a bitch a thing or two! I would have done this, and I would have done that. But one thing for sure, I would have gotten us out of that ticket.'

The sheriff concluded, "I'm now personally giving you the opportunity in advance to get everything off your chest. So go ahead, I'm listening."

I certainly frown upon the slapping scenario and hope that such instances never occur, but as with this fictitious local county sheriff, I never agreed with such statements about what people shoulda, coulda or woulda done after the fact. Armchair quarterbacks are a dime a dozen. As for me, I'm telling you from first-hand personal experience, no one knows for certain how he or she would have handled the charge of an enraged Brahma bull named Joe.

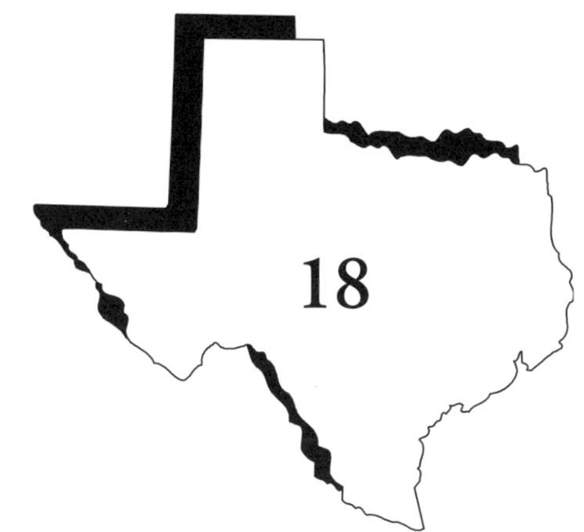

18

NARROW ESCAPES AND THE GREAT SNAKE CAPER

OUR WOODEN HOUSE AT CHINQUAPIN COULD never boast of a sensational security system because the windows and doors had neither screens nor functioning locks. Even though the outside doors were fitted with those old-fashioned square latches, the closures were completely useless because our keys had been lost years ago.

Since it never occurred to anyone in my family to change the mechanisms, the subject of protection became irrelevant. Such as it was, our personal property, therefore, lay extremely vulnerable because when we left home, thieves could easily enter the premises and take whatever they wanted. Dad, very stoic about the issue, said that it really didn't matter one way or the other;

we had nothing of value that anyone would want to steal in the first place.

Weather also influenced the whole process. Due to the extreme heat and high humidity during the summer and early autumn, we had no choice but to leave the windows open wide in order to survive the stifling temperatures. Since air conditioning was unheard of in our neck of the woods, I never thought much about the practice until a little later on when we learned about the potential hazards such action precipitated.

I started the first grade with a young lady named Betty Doyen, who came from a rather large family that included numerous brothers and sisters, most of them classmates. One morning as I took my seat on the bus, Harold Loggins asked me if I had heard about the Doyen's family fix. When I answered in the negative, he spared no details while relaying the blood-chilling events of the previous night. I found out that the Doyen's house had a security and cooling system similar to ours, and they had left their screenless windows open on that hot September evening.

During the previous year, the entire area suffered one of the worst rabies epidemics in recorded history. Livestock, raccoons, dogs, cats and foxes contended with this ancient misery, and our family eventually came face to face with the hideous affliction. One mid-day, Dad was busy driving some of our hogs from one side of the road to the other when a red fox ran out of the woods and jumped onto the back of one of our best sows. The fox held his ground and refused to retreat, even though Dad threw rocks at it and yelled at the top of his voice. Mom and I were inside the house when we heard all the commotion. Dad screamed instructions for Mom to bring his shotgun and be quick about it!

I stood in amazement and watched the fox continue the assault on the hog, and surprisingly, it displayed no fear at the sight of humans. *This was strange*, I thought, but at that juncture, I really knew nothing at all about the species. Even though I heard them barking during many a night, I had never seen a real fox before. I did know, however, that they were more or less nocturnal and elusive creatures; the reality of one operating in brought daylight seemed very peculiar.

Mom finally located the unloaded, single-barrel shotgun that stood in the corner closet. After inserting a shell, she hurriedly carried the weapon to Dad, who took deadly aim and promptly sent the fox to never-never land. When it was safe, I ran outside, and all of us stood around looking at the carcass.

Then Dad stated, "That rascal must have rabies—hydrophobia—for sure!"

As he examined the fox very carefully, he commented on the fact that it frothed at the mouth. That, he said, was a sure sign and proof positive of the animal's ailment. He added that he would have to put the hog down as well due to its injuries sustained while being attacked. Mom and I walked away and turned our eyes; we couldn't bear to look. Afterward, Dad took shovel in hand and buried both animals. He spoke in unknown terms: "If others devour these remains, they will get rabies as well" and "I'm sure glad that we did not get bitten!"

Later that night, I inquired about the initial stages and final result of such a horrific disease. "What would happen to a human if they got it?" I asked. "Would they die?"

Dad explained the final outcome. If shots were not taken soon after the bite or even a small scratch, an individual would suffer madness, followed by a terrible and excruciating death. He reiterated that after a certain point, no cure existed for the infectious ailment. Somewhere in that dire analysis, Dad mentioned also that animals could be protected only if they had been given rabies vaccinations. Those revelations sent shivers up my spine. We owned dogs and cats, and I knew that none of them had ever received any type of preventive medication. That's the way it was in those days; animals usually had to fend for themselves.

Naturally as a youngster, I played constantly with the household pets, and as a consequence received numerous scratches, though unintended, from Lep, my trusty hound, and Kitty Tom, my favorite feline. In reality, each could have been very easily infected with rabies, thereby spreading it to me. That worried me tremendously, even though I was only six years old.

The issue presented itself again and again. Almost every night we could hear the fox population bark and carry on in the woods very near to our house. I lay awake for hours on end, hoping and praying that one of the varmints would not elect to enter my bedroom window. That never happened to us, however, but the Doyen's family was not so lucky.

As Harold Loggins told the story on that morning, he explained that during the previous night, a rabid fox jumped into one of the Doyen kids' window and went plumb crazy. In total confusion, one after the other, family members attempted to remove the victim from the clutches of the wild beast. Finally, they were able to destroy the mad fox, but only after everyone had been wounded during the encounter. The neighbors were immediately summoned to transport the entire Doyen's family to the hospital in San Augustine where they received the first in a lengthy series of painful injections. I listened intently as Harold explained that the shots were plunged directly into the stomach region. Furthermore, he emphasized that the size of the needle was as big as a finger and its length measured more than a foot. *Good*

God, I thought. *If they don't die of hydrophobia, surely, the instrument will do them in!*

Those events did not contribute much toward my gaining a full and peaceful night's sleep. During the day, I either sat in school or at home, fearing whether one of those recent scratches by Lep or Kitty Tom might produce the fatal disease that would finally send me to death's door. Thinking back, this was a very traumatic experience in my young life. Nowadays, counselors, psychologists and other medical professionals would crawl out of the woodwork and provide the total school body and surrounding area with help in dealing with such a problem. But I suppose at the time, we were in many ways like the animals of our community—we had to fend for ourselves.

Personally, I endured various narrow escapes that could have ended my life prior to the age of ten because I strove constantly for bigger and more exciting adventures. In my opinion, the best source material could be found at the theater in San Augustine. Movies were always important to me, and I attended the show every chance I got. The heroes of the day came in the form of western stars such as Roy Rogers, Gene Autry, Hopalong Cassidy, Lash Larue, Randolph Scott, Bill Elliott, Charles Starrett, Tim Holt, Johnny Mack Brown, Tex Ritter—and the all-time jungle man, Tarzan. Now I'm not talking about all those other imposters. There is one and only Tarzan, and he came in the persona of Johnny Weismueller. Of course, other favorites included Flash Gordon and Buck Rogers, the precursor heroes to the Star Trek generation.

I sat many a Saturday from about 10:00 a.m. until 3:00 in the afternoon, marveling at the way Tarzan swung from tree to tree in the great African forests. Although Chinquapin sported some unusually fine underbrush, it never had anything remotely similar to a jungle. And even though grapevines were plentiful, Everett and I could never figure out how we could use them to fly through the trees. So we came upon the notion that maybe we could traverse the airways by an alternate method. After climbing a small pine sapling and using our weight to bend it toward another in the near distance, we would climb into the second tree, and so on.

Well, that seemed to be a good idea at the time! After several successful trial runs, Everett and I believed that we had worked out all the kinks—and everything seemed A-okay. So, as with the cigarette-smoking escapade, we agreed to try our tree climbing and bending shenanigans right there on campus. The other guys were invited to participate, the stage was set and the performance, so to speak, would occur at a clump of small pines located on the grounds near the entrance off the main road.

Before class started one morning, we scaled the trees like a band of monkeys. With each member of the corps perched atop his respective sapling, we began the maneuver with the grace and polish of a synchronized swimming team. At first, everyone, including me, realized extraordinary success, and I was thrilled to be a part of this history-making development. But on the second attempt, however, something went wrong! I assume that my tree was too small—instead of bending gently toward the second jumping off point, both craft and pilot fell full-speed toward the ground. I hit with a dull thud and immediately realized that the noise did not come from the tree itself, but from my foolish skull. Perhaps I now more clearly understood the term of break-neck speed.

I lay there, unable to move for the longest time. By now, one would think that I had become immune to such pain, but this was the worst yet. All my buddies came to my rescue, and each shared a common opinion that I had sustained a serious neck injury. One ran toward the schoolhouse to seek the aid of a teacher, while I continued to lie on the ground, groaning continuously. My neck hurt, and I had never experienced such throbbing agony from any source, either before or after. There was no faking here!

Aware that my recent antics might get me in trouble, not only with the teacher but also with my parents, I tried to stand ever so cautiously. When it seemed everything was in good working order, I was greatly relieved. However, when Mrs. Collins arrived on the scene, the tempo changed!

"What the heck were you thinking about," she scolded, "by attempting such a stupid exhibition?"

What could I say other than, "I don't know?"

Seeking desperately to throw her off track, I demonstrated that no aftereffects persisted, and she needn't worry. After repeating a few more questions, including the one about how would she be able to explain to our parents that we had broken our necks on school property, Mrs. Collins finally tired of our begging and agreed to keep all this business between us. So with a mere promise that we would never perform our "death-defying circus acts" again, she dropped the matter altogether. She must have been as happy as I was about the favorable ending.

But the intense pain in my head continued for several days after that. In retrospect, I probably had suffered a concussion, but who knows? I never told my parents about the incident, but years later when I began to experience serious headaches almost daily, my thoughts returned to that particular morning. Perhaps my tree climbing and falling days finally caught up with me.

Chinquapin was home to many types of slithering critters, including that granddaddy of all spiders, the tarantula, as well as various species of snakes that seemingly appeared at every turn. I always steered clear of all reptiles and recently have come to believe that I have a lot in common with Indiana Jones, the great archeologist whose character graced films such as *The Temple of Doom* and *Raiders of the Lost Ark*. There is a particular scene in the latter, when Indy and a sidekick peered into a chamber that housed the long-sought religious symbol. His friend asked why the floor moved, and upon closer inspection, both noted that it was the writhing of thousands of snakes.

Indy said, "Snakes! Why does it always have to be snakes?" These words express my exact sentiments and I'll tell you why.

During the second grade, Dad and I arrived at Daddy Wright's old place to do some squirrel hunting. With Dad out of sight, I looked around to find something to occupy my time and spied a huge apple tree, brimming with fruit, near the side of the house.

Naturally, I could not leave without experiencing the nectar of the gods, so I scurried up the tree in search of the perfect apple. The few closer ones did not catch my attention, so I climbed higher until I finally saw the one that I really wanted. As I neared the top, I remained focused on the ultimate prize. When I reached for the fruit, however, I noticed a slight movement above me. Jolted by my worst fears, I stared directly into the eyes of the largest and ugliest snake that I had ever seen personally, no more than five or six inches away from me.

Sometimes, I am told that physical forces beyond explanation take over in the face of catastrophic events, and people are able to perform superhuman feats for a brief time. I suppose that's what happened to me. I'll never know how high I ascended on that particular occasion, but no matter; I didn't take the time to worry about anything other than that snake. With everything considered, however, I decided that he could have my apple along with the entire crop. After all he was there first, and he appeared very comfortable in the lush surroundings. The tree was not big enough for both of us, so one had to go!

After determining that I had a better chance of surviving a fall rather than snakebite directly to the face, I made a quick choice. Without hesitation, I turned loose of the branch that supported my weight and fell backward. The last thing I recall is that I hit the ground running toward my dad, announcing my latest predicament with as much exaggeration as possible. Dad placed his shotgun in ready position and ran toward me. He looked upward to where I pointed, laughed and explained that the terror that loomed so large only moments before was nothing more than a small, harmless green tree snake, which was probably more afraid of me than I of him.

"No," I replied. "That's not the same snake! The one I saw was much larger—even bigger than the boa constrictor that almost killed Tarzan."

It took quite a while for me to come to terms with that dilemma. And you can only imagine where my mind drifted each time I heard various Baptist preachers offer religious interpretations about Adam and Eve and their Garden of Eden encounter with the serpent in a tree. Even though I never expressed my private observations to anyone, for years I thought that perhaps I had come across that *same* snake, of all places, in Chinquapin, Texas.

Speaking of heights, I have never been particularly fond of those either, even though I loved to climb trees. But I did, however, set reasonable and responsible limits to distances of at least thirty feet, about the same as the roof system on the Chinquapin school building. During the time of the Korean War, the structure's roofing material, consisting of sheets of tin, had become severely rusted and required a new paint job. Dad said that he could use the extra money, so he submitted a successful bid for the contract to apply new silver coating to the entire surface. As luck would have it, he started during the month of July, on some of the hottest days that I could ever recall.

I WAS HERE FIRST!

Now my father was not one to dawdle; he wanted to finish everything as quickly as possible. If it took a normal person three months to do something, Dad did it in two. Furthermore, he did not like to deal with unnecessary interruptions, so he intended to complete this project prior to the school opening in September. He didn't want all those kids around bothering him while he worked.

I went with Dad to the job at every opportunity, but each time Mom made him swear an oath that he wouldn't allow me to scramble up the ladder that thirty feet or so to the top of the roof. That worked well at first, but after several days, I finally talked Dad into letting me give it a try. Again, I pledged that I would be extra careful and never, under any circumstances, would I get too near the wet paint. Dad explained if that happened, a strong possibility existed that I would slide off the side of the building and plunge thirty feet below to an untimely death.

The concept of falling scared the hell out of me at first, but not enough for me to maintain a careful posture on an extended basis. I got used to being way up there very quickly, so I began taking unnecessary chances. With Dad busy on the other side of the roof and out of sight, I decided to trot and then run as fast as I could. When I did, I realized that I could not stop before reaching a freshly painted section. Just as Dad predicted, I fell flat on my butt and began sliding toward the edge. I experienced more terror during those moments than during my entire lifetime, regardless of what I might have said earlier. Lying on my posterior and seeing nothing but blue sky and thin air approaching rapidly, I sped onward.

I used every trick I could think of to slow my momentum, but nothing worked, and I continued on the course of certain doom. For some reason known only to God Almighty, I stopped about two feet from the brink. I struggled to my feet, and finally succeeded in locating a dry spot from which to make my escape. With safety at hand, the endless possibilities I had just escaped hit me like a ton of bricks. I stood there trembling, with tears in my eyes. After gaining my composure, I found the ladder and stepped downward to safety.

When Dad stopped for lunch, he noticed the paint on the rear of my overalls and asked how it got there. I hesitated to tell the truth, but after hearing one of those statements that parents are known for—"Now don't you lie to me!"—I confessed that I had almost met my maker. Hearing that disclosure, Dad administered swift and immediate justice by applying a few stiff slaps to my rear section. I really didn't mind at all, because I was just happy to be able to feel them. By the way, I never wanted to go back upon that roof again, and I didn't.

But as time wore on, I began to brag about how I was able to elude the Grim Reaper, and when school started, I pointed out the site of my near demise to several attentive friends. Each marveled at the height and my latest tale, but soon, I'm sure that I was the only person who cared to remember.

We raised poultry on our farm, and like most rural families of the time, we ate a lot of fried chicken for lunch on Sundays. Of course we depended upon the birds for other things besides the means by which to attract the preacher and his family after church—namely, the fowl provided us with a steady supply of eggs.

When we bought the farm, it came equipped with what we referred to as a chicken coop, located a few yards directly behind our house. The coop, nothing more than a small building, contained several elevated stalls with nests for the layers to occupy while producing their eggs. Each day, either Mom or Dad went to the chicken house and gathered the current output.

The fenced area surrounding our coop had been the location of many hair-raising events. Once a fox managed to gain entry, and after creating a lot of havoc, he captured one of our pullets. With old Lep hot on his heels, the varmint narrowly escaped into the nearby woods. During another equally exciting session, some type of hawk, surely a chicken hawk, landed in the yard and carried off its prey. But all those paled in comparison to the time that Mom came face to face with an unsuspecting competitor.

For those of you who are unfamiliar with chicken yards, I must explain that more species than humans appreciate the taste of fresh-laid eggs. By necessity, Dad reminded us that we had to be on the constant lookout for egg suckers, dogs that ate eggs. Farmers had little use for these scamps, and usually dispelled them to other worlds without giving it a second thought. Dad said once that when a dog got his first taste of an egg, he or she became totally useless. Rendered incapable of work and having lost the desire to hunt, these wayward creatures spent all day and night trying to satisfy their cravings. Dad remarked that they were drawn to eggs as bees are to honey! I always doubted the validity of this old tale, but just to be on the safe side, I tried to keep all my dogs, including Lep, away from the hallowed and sanctified chicken headquarters.

One spring morning, while Dad worked in the field, Mom and I attended to other chores, including milking the cows, feeding the chickens and gathering eggs. Actually I contributed very little, but I was awfully good at just hanging around and getting in the way. With all duties completed except one, Mom and I walked into the chicken house.

Mom is about five feet and four inches, and in order to reach the nests and their clutches of eggs, she had to stand on her toes with hands outstretched. As she did this, she let out a series of blood-curdling screams. I ran toward her and noticed that she stood frozen, while yelling gibberish at the top of her voice. I became alarmed and asked her what was wrong.

She explained frantically that she had hold of a snake. I imagined that the reptile must have buried his giant fangs into her hand and that she would surely die. Quickly remembering my personal run-in with the serpent in the apple tree, I suggested that she let go, but she remarked that she *could not*. To me, that statement was as empty as a water bucket with a hole in it the size of a four-bit piece, but whatever the explanation, nothing impaired Mom's voice, which remained intact and in top-notch condition. She shouted for me to get a hoe. I ran toward the house and returned with the instrument, knowing full well the eventual outcome. Mom continued to scream and I stood there helpless!

After several minutes, she gained some measure of self-control and began pulling that reptile, the longest that I ever saw up to that time, from the nest. He had swallowed every egg in the nest and was so full that he could barely move. Added to that, I'm sure that he must have been disoriented by the free-for-all. Only then did I learn that snakes, as well as some dogs, love to eat eggs.

Mom finally came to her senses. She let loose of the snake and proceeded to deliver him to the happy hunting ground with the hoe. When I asked why she did not let go, she explained how fear prevented her from moving. At the time, I thought this a crock of—absurdity!

Two lessons resulted from the experience with that unfortunate chicken snake. One should never put a hand in a dark and forebidding place because you can't see what's in there. Some folks, and especially Steve Irwin, better known as *The Crocodile Hunter*, have yet to learn from Mom's mistake and her subsequent demonstration. Second, be slow to criticize others for making poor choices because one never really has the faintest clue what he or she will do until being confronted by identical circumstances. I found out the second part later on when Joe, our Brahma bull, gave chase and almost put me in an early grave.

You can discover what your enemy fears most by observing the means he uses to frighten you.

—Eric Hoffer

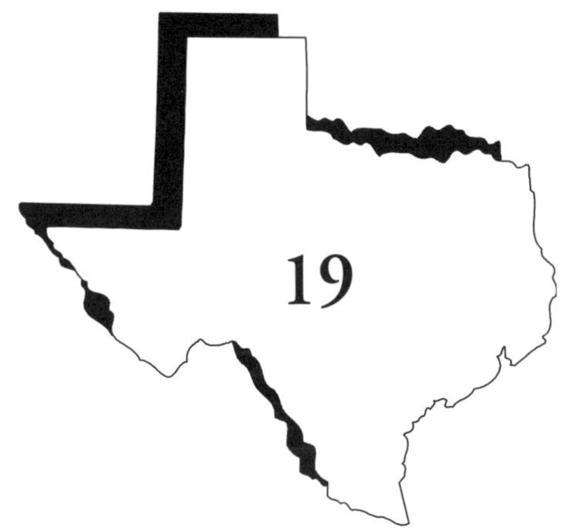

NEW VOCABULARY

UNTIL THE SIXTH GRADE, I HAD ALWAYS WEATH-ered the personal storms that came my way, no matter how severe. I was able to smoke cigarettes without destroying either the barn or the school building. Once I partook of a large plug of Brown Mule chewing tobacco, and soon thereafter, I accepted the likelihood that I might die of its effects. But of course, I didn't. I never shot myself with the Stevens single-shot .22 rifle, never put my eye out with the Daisy BB gun that I received one Christmas, had never been mauled or gored by a bull, nor had I been hurt in an automobile accident.

Numerous bee stings, bouts with wasp nests, bumble-bees and scorpions had failed to do me in. Furthermore, I received no more than a good scare after eating poi-soned green tomatoes, and I beat back the assaults generated by two medical enigmas: seed warts and the sudden onset of stuttering. At age four and without anyone knowing, I took several aspirins after complaining of a terrible headache. Later that same day, I found out that, much to the regret of my internal organs, the pain medication belonged to Dad who received the prescription after he suffered a back Injury at the Bethlehem Shipyard in Beaumont. I managed a full recovery from that development as well.

I had never received a snake bite, never been seriously bitten by a dog or cat, and I never required so much as one stitch to close numerous gaping wounds occurring on most parts of my extremities. While helping Dad stretch a fence around some recently cleared new ground, I escaped a devastating injury when my arm became entangled in a broken and snarled strand of barbed wire. I also survived, without noticeable scars, a burning nightshirt incident when I backed into a butane heater on a cold winter night.

I had been to the dentist twice in my lifetime. Back then, we only made those visits when a tooth began to hurt and needed pulling. Dad, quick on the draw, extracted my first loose tooth with some fencing pliers, and then both of us returned to work. Neither had I suffered a single broken limb from various falls from tree-climbing antics. That possibility always held some intrigue, however, seeing my buddies in casts with all those signatures and statements from enthusiasts.

Always extremely lucky, I even finished the first day of school without bodily harm, and never in any of my academic past had I received more than one lick of corporal punishment, despite all the fights and trouble in which I had become embroiled. I suppose much of that good fortune lay in the fact that I made good grades, which endeared me to the hearts of various teachers throughout my school years.

During the last half of the sixth grade, however, I learned that certain aspects of education received from life experiences and on the school campus were not necessarily accepted at home, to say the least. Nothing had prepared me for what soon followed.

Nolan Ainsworth had always been a very close friend. Although he was one grade ahead of me, that didn't matter at all. I viewed him as somewhat of a role model and hoped sooner or later to walk in his footsteps. Nolan's dad owned a general store, and even though he never laid direct claim, Preston Ainsworth must have also been in the junk business. The Ainsworths' back yard held many riches, including discarded auto parts, batteries, iceboxes, washing machines, lawn mowers and such. Nolan used many of these castoffs to construct one of those cars that we read about that ran in the Boxcar Derby.

Since the Ainsworth house perched on the side of a steep slant, Nolan and I put the topography to good use and formed a neat racetrack. While dreaming that one day we would compete in the national finals, we spent hours piloting our car through the curves meandering around giant shade trees and the posts that supported the home's structure,

Now I didn't mention it earlier, but Nolan, a big rawboned blonde kid, also inherited the gift of gab from his father. Looking back, I think that Nolan and comedian Rodney Dangerfield had a lot in common. Every morning, whether on the school bus or on the playground, Nolan would express the same thing: "Boy, I don't feel good today."

That served as the cue. I'd respond, "I'm sorry, Nolan. What's the matter now?"

Then he'd remark, "I'm not sure, but I've picked up a disease since yesterday, and it's got me down bad."

"What do you think it is?" I'd ask.

"As close as I can tell," he said, "it might be the Senigens" (pronounced sen-i-ghins).

Now those not properly schooled in medical jargon may not know about the Senigens. Nolan claimed that this was being down in one's back—and too, there were other afflictions such as the Hitidaritis (hi-tida-ritus) which he related as severe leg cramps, and the Bohunkus (bohunk-us), a stressful malady associated with a sore butt. Nolan complained of those imaginary diseases on a daily basis to many fans on the schoolyard, who howled with laughter and praise.

Although he never explained fully where he learned those words, I always assumed that he made them up. Nevertheless, I thought them extremely noteworthy, and never being one to shirk family responsibility, I tried them out on my mom.

For months on end upon my daily arrival from school, Mom and I entertained the disease-of-the-day joke. She would inquire of my health, and in turn I'd advise her of my most current problem, whether it be the Senigens, Hitidaritis or the Bohunkus. Mom went along with the jokes, laughed and seemed to enjoy these diseases as much as I did. However, things were to change all too soon. One morning at school during the first recess, Nolan called me aside, where he promptly announced that he had heard of two entirely new illnesses. He mentioned that he had become tired of using the same old weary lines and for the sake of variety, he sought out some new terminology.

I thought this a very smart plan and waited with anticipation to learn something about the new ailments. "Come on, Nolan," I asked, "what are they?"

"The gonorrhea and the syphilis!"

Boy, won't this be great? I thought. *Mom will surely get a kick out of these, especially since she's probably as exhausted as we are of hearing the same medical terms.*

All during that day I busied myself telling all my class-mates about my new medical problems, and one by one, my buddies squealed with delight as I repeated the terms upon second and third requests. I could hardly wait for the school bus to deliver me at home. I jumped from the seat and ran into the house, where I found Mom in the kitchen preparing one of her scrumptious chocolate pud-dings. Before she turned around, I delivered my expected line. "Gee, Mom, I'm feeling especially bad today. I'm suffering from two new diseases."

She laughed and asked, "What is it this time?"

"I've got a bad case of the gonorrhea!" I said.

Mom dropped her spoon, and before she said a word, I responded with the second shot to the bow. "And that's not all. I've also got the syphilis." This brought a scream.

Now I had received sighs, laughter and sometimes only smiles on a bad delivery, but never had I caught a reaction that sounded like that. I thought this peculiar in-deed, but who knows about that fickle thing called com-edy?

During the following moments Mom acted even more strangely. She turned, dropped to her knees, grabbed my shoulders and stared into my eyes with one of *those looks*. I knew that things were not quite right, but I also knew I had done nothing wrong that day. At least that's what I thought up to that point.

True to form, Mom began the interrogation process. The questions and answers came in rapid-fire succession:

"Where?"

"School."

"Who taught them to you?"

"Nolan."

"And who heard you repeat them?"

"The entire school body, if they had taken the time to listen."

"The whole school! My God, what will they think of us?"

"Nothing," I said. "They already know about the Senigens, Hitidaritis and Bohunkus."

That must have been the wrong thing to say, because Mom walked into the bedroom, where she retrieved one of Dad's belts from the bedpost. After a few swift licks, Mom finally gained enough self-control to explain about these vulgar words and how they were affiliated with social misfortunes. She added something about men, women and sex, but I really had no idea what she was talking about. She saw that she was fighting a losing battle, and left it to Dad. Later he graphically explained the potential problem areas in relation to the male anatomy. After that discussion, I knew one thing for sure. I wanted no part of the syphilis or the gonorrhea.

Dad attempted to maintain a straight face, but he smiled at me while Mom wrote one of her famous notes to my teacher, this one outlining her case about how this was all a serious misunderstanding and how we were really good people who did not carry those types of diseases. The next morning Mrs. Smith accepted the note with grace and explained that Mom and Dad were not really suspect. Again I had to promise never to speak those words again, especially in school.

When next I saw Nolan, I informed him about my latest situation and how he had caused all sorts of trouble for me. I counseled that he should not use the words either, for fear of reprimand, but he openly expressed amusement at the incident and continued as if nothing ever happened.

After a couple of weeks the whole thing died down, and Mom let me resume the visits to Nolan's house, where he promptly sold me two rabbits—a buck and doe. Unfortunately, the latter turned out to be another buck, so my disease epidemic ended about the same time as my best-laid plans of becoming a prosperous rabbit farmer.

New Vocabulary

I am reminded of the two young brothers who decided that they were old enough to begin cursing. One decided to use a favorite word, *hell*, and the other determined his word of choice to be *ass*. One Saturday morning they developed a plan. Words of such great stature are wasted unless properly shared with an audience. At breakfast they would try their respective words on their mother.

When the brothers arrived at the breakfast table, the mother looked to the younger son and asked what he wanted to eat. "Ah, hell," he answered with glee. "I suppose I'll try some of those Crunchie-Munchies."

The mother promptly jerked the boy from his seat, applied a slap to his behind and sent him crying to his room without breakfast. She then turned to the older son and with a stern look, posed the same question. The boy thought carefully before responding, "I'm not sure, Mom, but you can bet your sweet ass that I don't want any of those Crunchie-Munchies!"

Now my lesson learned was similar to that of the unsuspecting brothers. I cannot tell you that I never in the future used words not fully understood by me, but you can be assured of one thing. I never again repeated to my mother those dreaded social terms of syphilis and gonorrhea.

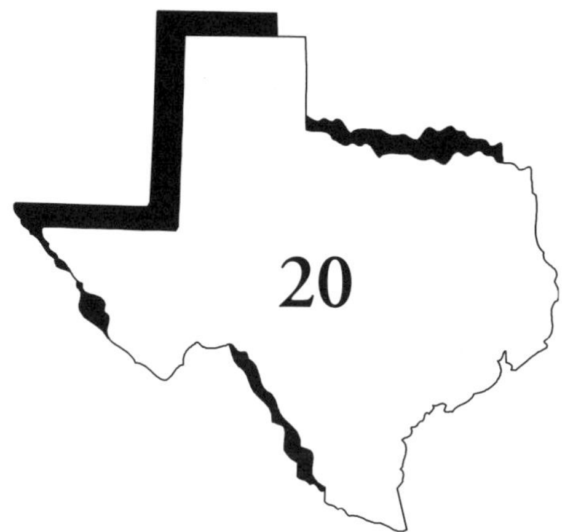

20

WHAT'S MINE IS MINE

EING AN ONLY CHILD, I NEVER WORRIED ABOUT sharing my toys and other playthings. This also applied to my most favorite dessert in the entire universe—chocolate pudding. I don't remember whether Mom made it every day, but she came close. No meal was complete without it. In fact, I ate it for snacks at about two p.m. during lazy summer days, while Mom enjoyed a steaming cup of coffee.

Once my cousin, Tudor, and Aunt Johnnie B. came by our house and interrupted this afternoon ritual. We had just finished a late lunch, and I was about to start on my pudding when the visitors arrived. Mom instructed me to place the dessert in the icebox, or if I wanted, I could share the tasty morsel with my younger guest.

I responded with an emphatic, "No way," and before the relatives made it to the kitchen, I put the pudding on the bottom shelf, way toward the back, behind the jelly jars and butter dish, out of plain view. As they say in the criminal profession, the goods would most certainly be safe from any improperly executed search warrants.

All retired to the living room and took our respective positions. Tudor turned to me and suggested that we go out and play. My thoughts, however, returned to the chocolate pudding. By my telling him no, I concluded that maybe he would tire of just sitting and ask that his mother take him home—but no such luck. We sat, sat and then sat some more.

Finally I thought, *It doesn't look like they're ever going to leave, and I've got to have some of that pudding!*

After several restless minutes I devised a plan, filled with stealth and genius. I would make some excuse, return to the kitchen, retrieve my bowl of pudding, place it behind my back and go back to the living room. While Tudor wasn't looking, I would reach behind, take a spoonful and place it in my mouth very carefully. I thought that no one would ever catch on.

I began the operation. Initially, everything went extremely well—I was able to sit in the forward part of the chair with the bowl perched nicely at my back. Savoring the first spoonful ever so cleverly, I remained undetected through the next couple of bites—but old Tudor knew something was up!

"What are you eating?" he asked.

"Nothing, why?"

He looked at my aunt and made a request for whatever I was having. Mom, a little embarrassed by the incident, issued instructions about getting another container and letting Tudor have some. She added that I should be ashamed of myself, but I failed to see the necessity of such a solemn and excessive move. After all, this pudding belonged to me, so I uttered, "No!"

"If you can't divide," Mom rebuked, "then put it up! We'll talk about this later."

I knew what that meant—another spanking, most probably—but it was worth the torture to prevent sharing that nectar of the gods. Aunt Johnnie B. and my cousin left in a huff, feeling a little bit insulted, but as far as I was concerned, this was good riddance. For obvious reason, I was more than happy to see them go.

As expected, Mom expressed complete disappointment in my latest actions, but shortly I convinced her that this would never happen again. She accepted my word, and I was allowed to finish that bowl of chocolate pudding, which remained waiting, undefiled. Happy days returned once more.

Now this was not the lone instance that I found myself deeply immersed in boiling water over the inability to share. It happened later, but this time the consequences could have resulted in serious injury, not to mention problems associated with a burning sensation on the bottom half of my body.

To begin with, I need to explain how the situation developed. Our family owned a dog named Lep. Once I asked about the origin of that strange name, to which Dad responded with some twaddle about how the big scalawag took on a leopard by himself without gaining so much as a minor scratch. All this allegedly occurred on some wild African safari. I really didn't give credence to the story, but it sounded good just the same. Besides, my dad seemed to enjoy recounting Lep's spectacular deed, which became more embellished with each telling.

There was, however, another more believable version, most probably nearer to the actual truth. It seemed that Dad got the old hound in some trade, but he also got the raw end of the deal when he found out later that the acquisition had a bad skin condition, namely the red mange. My uncle said that the hound's scarred complexion reminded Dad of a leper in biblical times, so he decided to shorten the name and simply call him Lep.

At any rate, I loved that dog dearly. We became inseparable, and I came to view him as the brother I never had. We played Tarzan together. I took the Tarzan role of course, and Lep became the wild animal that I always

WHO SAID VOLUNTEER?
I WAS DRAFTED!
LEP
RED FLYER
CALVIN BLASSINGAME

managed to subdue. Numerous times, both Dad and Mom threatened to get rid of the pooch unless I stopped wrestling with him. They were afraid that I would catch the mange, but even that possibility failed to deter me. After all, he and I were the best of friends, and one should never desert a faithful companion.

One Christmas, Santa Claus presented me with one of the prettiest red wagons that you've ever seen. With that Radio Flyer, Lep and I had the greatest times. I would imagine Lep as the test pilot who volunteered to ride his craft down the red-dirt hill above our house. And so he did, but I might add that the term "volunteer" had nothing to do with it. I strapped him into the wagon, tied the handle to maintain a straight trajectory and started it on the perilous jaunt.

At the time I thought this situation hilarious. There he was—Lep in the red wagon, going down the hill like a bat out of Hades, his ears flapping in the breeze and barking in what I imagine now was a canine's way of expressing out-and-out fright. He was a real trooper, though, because when the wagon stopped, either by loss of speed or being turned on its side, he remained put. Then I pulled the Radio Flyer back up the hill with its cargo intact, repeating the process time after time. I realize that some may criticize my actions in this escapade as cruel and unusual punishment, but at least I had the forethought to provide my buddy with a seat belt for his protection. I never had one of those for myself until 1965, some seventeen years later.

Other days Lep and I whiled away the time playing in the cool, moist dirt underneath our house which stood on blocks. Mom and Dad often cautioned me about my play location, but I was sure if snakes, lizards or other deadly creatures placed me in harm's way, my sidekick would surely protect me.

Now, let's return to the original theme. One Sunday afternoon my mother's brother, Paul, his wife and their three children stopped for a visit. Because the Wright family lived in San Augustine, I always considered my two older cousins, Giles and Frances Jean, as city slickers, in that they were not very adept at finding things to occupy their time, at least in my rural setting. However, I didn't hold the youngest daughter, Betty Ruth, who was still a baby, to those higher standards.

In a matter of minutes Frances Jean grew bored of doing nothing. She walked into our back yard and found my homemade swing, consisting of a rough piece of board suspended from a limb by two frayed and uneven rope snippets, located at the base of a large white oak tree. I wasn't using the contraption, nor had I any plans to, but the mental picture of someone else playing there, having a jolly good old time, was completely repugnant and beyond all comprehension.

When I ordered that she get out of it, she used that familiar expression of children throughout the ages: "I don't have to. Make me!"

I had always been a great fan of the movies and talked my dad into letting me attend the Augus Theater in San Augustine whenever possible. I enjoyed western movies the most, but another favorite choice revolved around the knights of old. Many times I imagined myself as Sir Galahad or one of the other members of King Arthur's Round Table with all accouterments, clothing and arms, involved in fierce and deadly jousting matches. The favorite adversary, of course, was the Black Knight. In order to make my fantasies more realistic, I had cut down a slender pine sapling, removed the bark and fashioned it into my own lance with which to fend off the evils of the kingdom. I rounded out the armaments with a shield cut from two wide boards nailed together, painted white and topped off with a large black initial M to reflect the family insignia.

With Frances Jean swinging, without approval, and my weapon in plain sight, I sprang into action. I grabbed the lance and shield, mounted my stick horse and proceeded to dislodge my cousin, the Black Knight, from her saddle. I now realize that the whole matter is a little far fetched, and I suppose that this is one of those repre-sentative occasions best described as you just had to be there.

Frances Jean stood no chance in this contest of wills. I aimed skillfully, charged—and to my complete surprise, she fell to the ground. *Boy, this is great,* I thought. *Mission accomplished.*

However, when Frances Jean arose, blood gushed from beneath the hands that covered her face. She screamed and ran toward the porch where my parents and relatives were engaged in busy conversation. Only then did the terror hit me. At the outset, I thought that I had put out her eye. If true, I knew that all hell would soon break loose.

Then I heard my aunt scream, after which the entire enclave rushed toward the back—looking for me! I was a marked man who had to think fast. Leaning on experi-ence, I remembered hiding under the house after dump-ing dirt in the water buckets carried by Aunt Georgia Mae Parrish. This maneuver saved my bacon that day, and it could very well work again. So with a large enemy force bearing down on me, I did what most self-respecting knights should have done when faced with a superior foe. I ran for cover!

I barely made it to the edge of the house to slide underneath toward the middle part and safety, at least for the moment. However, it was touch and go. Hands tugged at my feet, but I was able to shake loose, break free and escape. Over the next few minutes I endured all types of threats imaginable, beginning with my dad, who vowed that he would whip the living daylights out of me, and then from Aunt Lizzie, who scolded me for coming too close to her daughter's eye. Then I knew that she must be okay and I began feeling a little smug about how I eluded capture. Frances Jean suffered some blood loss, but if she had only listened to me in the first place, this debacle could have been avoided.

With the discovery that my cousin bore no irreversible injury, I thought that everything should be forgiven, but unfortunately I was the only party who saw it that way. Thus, I remained in position and decided to wait out the siege. Lep, my one true remaining friend, crawled near, licked my face, lay down beside me and kept me company during the entire ordeal. Many times before, I had played in this identical spot, but never in the waning hours. Considering that nightfall swiftly approached, I began to think about the multitude of menacing varmints. I wasn't really sure whether old Lep was up to the task, no matter how strongly advertised.

I became extremely pleased when, one by one, my attackers lost faith and withdrew. Only Mom remained steadfast. When I heard the sound of my uncle's car crank and then fade into the distance, I felt that I had gained a more favorable bargaining chip, so I began to play on Mom's emotions. I pleaded with her to let me surrender with dignity, without having to experience either a switch or a belt to the backside. I told her that I had learned my lesson and that she should forgive as always. I argued, "I only protected what was mine!"

At the beginning of these skilled negotiations, Mom wouldn't entertain such nonsense, but when dusk turned to the dark of night, she finally relented. I guess that she also thought about those snakes and such, so she promised to spare the rod. I responded gladly, but I had not completely avoided the wrath—and for the next few hours I heard one of the sternest lectures yet. I concluded that maybe the licks would have been a better choice.

Anyway, I had a long time to think about what I had done before I scrambled to the refuge of the outside world. All of a sudden, the idea of sharing seemed to be accepted with more understanding and enthusiasm. Furthermore, Lep would not always be there to protect me. As it turned out, I was more of a visionary than anticipated. When the dog's skin problem rapidly deteriorated, Dad begged me to change my play habits—to maintain a safety zone—but he might as well have directed the mighty Mississippi to alter its course. Uncle John McCary showed up a few months later, but before leaving, however, he took a small rope and attached it to Lep's collar. As the two walked to the truck parked alongside the roadway, the old hound looked back over his shoulder and said goodbye in the only way that he knew how. That was the last time that I ever saw either of them. Even though Dad commented that it was for the best, things would never again be the same.

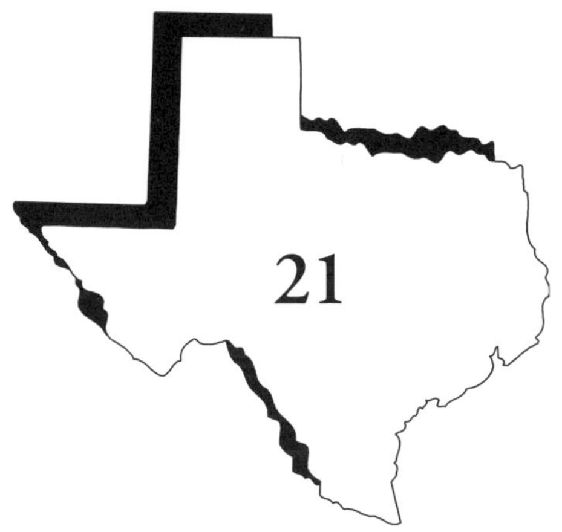

21

DADDY WRIGHT AND THE CRICKET

M Y MATERNAL GRANDFATHER, LLOYD NAPO-
leon Wright, always hated his middle name,
so he shortened it to Pony. Even though he
never legally changed it, he always signed his name as
L. P. Wright. Heaven help future researchers who are unfamiliar with his rationale and attempt to trace our family
tree!

From all accounts, my mom's parents had one of the
most prosperous farms in the Chinquapin area, which not
only supported the family of seven, but also produced
other material benefits. The Wrights were among the original recipients of telephone service in this part of the
county, even though the lines of communication connected to a mere handful of member households. Due

to a limited subscriber base that never expanded, the company finally went out of business prior to 1926. The service was slow to make its return—it would be another thirty-two years, about 1957, before residents of Chinquapin were able to hold telephone conversations over a party-line system that held little privacy.

Daddy Wright, as the grandchildren called him, also owned one of the first automobiles in Chinquapin. Mom disclosed that when in her teens, her father hitched a ride to San Augustine where he paid the astonishing sum of $500 for one of those shiny black Model-T Fords. Without any experience behind the wheel but with the grace of God, he managed to traverse the eight miles in between and arrive home without killing either himself or a poor innocent along the way. Immediately thereafter, he took the wife and kids for a demonstration tour that turned sour. Mom reported that he just about scared everyone half to death as he drove along the single-lane red-dirt roads, weaving from side to side, attempting to stay clear of the deep ditches. All family members breathed a sigh of relief when they got home in one piece that afternoon, and each of the five children vowed never to ride with Papa again.

Once I asked Mom whether Daddy Wright ever took a driving test to obtain an operator's license. She laughed and replied that he bought his at a drugstore in San Augustine. I questioned this statement at great length, but Mom reiterated that at one time this practice was entirely legal. She also offered the fact that Daddy Wright had never received any type of formal education in handling a moving vehicle. That really showed! Even in his younger years, my grandfather viewed the center stripe in a roadway as a guide, and instead of improving as he aged, I do believe that he got worse. He drove most times straddling the line that divided the two lanes, only to move over with the appearance of approaching traffic. Too, Daddy Wright never quite understood or appreciated speed limits. No, I'm not implying that he broke the law by exceeding the posted numbers. To the contrary, he never drove more than twenty miles an hour in his entire life, no matter how many cars and trucks stacked up behind him, with horns blowing and drivers yelling and waving for him to pull over and get out of the way.

Daddy Wright owned an old army jeep for years, and I remember how proud he was when he decided that it was time to buy something a little more modern and comfortable. He came by our house one afternoon on his way home, after going to San Augustine where he took delivery of a brand spanking new dark green 1951 Chevrolet pickup. He kept it for years, and in fact, it was the last vehicle that he ever owned. Daddy Wright never considered throwing money away on another transport just because the old one's paint had lost much of its luster and its seats had become a little ragged and torn. I guess that you could say that the old man was environmentally friendly. Furthermore, he never believed that outward appearances interfered with the performance of a motor—his motto: If it ain't broke, don't fix it.

I rode with Daddy Wright on numerous occasions, and each run ended with my confession that he drove like no other I had witnessed, either before or since. Once I remarked to Mom how he'd sit almost on top of the steering wheel, with both hands attached and holding on for dear life. Mom concluded that Papa never drove anything—he *herded* it.

Most times when we were along, he would hand the keys to Dad and ask him to take the controls. But after a few minutes, Daddy Wright requested that Dad slow down when he reached the perilous twenty-mile per hour marker. He didn't want to take any unnecessary chances that might lead to a collision, plus he didn't want to burn up the engine. After all, that Chevrolet truck had years of service left. My grandfather always practiced what he preached; he had much more time than money.

One afternoon in particular, we had taken him on an errand to San Augustine. As usual, Dad slid into the driver's seat, and by the time we got on the road to Chinquapin, darkness had set in. Shortly after leaving town,

Daddy Wright posed the question, "Do you boys hear that noise?"

"Noise? What noise?" we responded.

"I don't know quite how to describe it," he replied. "Maybe a chirp or something like that, but I'm not really sure. Anyway, I'll let you know when, and if, I hear it again."

Much to our sorrow, that question-and-answer session continued for the next eight miles. Daddy Wright constantly expressed a fear that something must have happened to the engine, and he hoped that we arrived home before the truck finally broke down and left us stranded. He did not relish the thought of our walking any great distance to seek assistance, given that the sky was extremely overcast and the remote country road, nearly pitch black. Secondly, no one knew what dangers lay at each of its flanks; the thick underbrush provided cover for a myriad of hostile possibilities. My granddad recounted that old-timers used to report about hearing panthers scream like banshees around these parts, and he claimed to have heard one also, when driving a wagon back from San Augustine years before. The fearful outcry caused the mules to panic, and he nearly lost the wagon in a creek bed before regaining control of the team. I must admit that after hearing that, I got a little spooked myself.

Soon we met an oncoming automobile, and about that time, Daddy Wright insisted that he heard the noise again. For the umpteenth time, Dad asked him what it sounded like. I wanted to know if he thought it might be one of those banshees.

"No," Daddy Wright said, "I'm talking about the other thing. Why, I believe it's a cricket."

Dad, growing more impatient at the constant discussion of unknown disturbances, had just about had all that he could stand. So he stopped the truck and directed that everyone get out and look for that stowaway cricket. With flashlights in hand, we searched every nook and cranny, every conceivable hideout, but to no avail. We never found the culprit responsible for the racket, so we got back into the truck and proceeded homeward.

Before long, Daddy Wright raised the alarm flag once more. He couldn't let the subject go and continued the onslaught as we pulled into our driveway. About that time, Dad dimmed the lights. For those of you who are accustomed to driving newer automobiles with the dimmer switch located on the steering column, you may not know or remember that manufacturers once placed those devices on the floorboards to the left of the clutch and brake pedals. The driver simply applied pressure on the switch with his or her left foot, which in turn produced alternate high- or low-beam headlights.

WHERE'S THAT CRICKET?

When Dad dimmed the lights and prepared to stop, my grandfather raised his voice and repeated, "See there, I heard it again. It went *click, click.*"

Almost simultaneously, Dad and I identified the source of my grandfather's long-standing complaint. "Mr. Pony," Dad remarked, "that's the dimmer switch. That's probably what you heard all the way home."

To our mutual bewilderment, Daddy Wright asked, "Dimmer...switch. What's a dimmer switch?"

This question caught us completely off guard. At first I thought it amusing and downright stupid for him, after considerable seasoning behind the wheel, to know nothing about a dimmer switch, something so basic to the art of driving. His own ten-year-old grandson knew its intended purpose, and so should he. I began to snicker, and Dad soon joined in.

Daddy Wright, however, found no humor in our laughter. To him, this represented a serious situation. He wanted to know what the heck Dad was talking about. As we pulled to a stop, Dad pointed toward the switch. He patiently explained its purpose of rotating from high beam headlights to low in order to prevent blinding the drivers of oncoming vehicles. Dad added that if one came too close without performing this procedure, others often called for the switch by blinking their lights several times.

The old man listened intently. Dad asked him whether he had ever noticed that little round thing on the floorboard? Daddy Wright responded that he had seen it for years, but he had never given it much thought.

"Now that you mention it," he acknowledged, "I do recall that sometimes at night, cars have blinked their lights at me. I always wondered what caused the flickering, but I suspected that maybe they had a short in their wires."

Dad and I got out of the truck, and I stood there, smiling, looking at this gentle being bare heart and soul about his limited knowledge of driving. Daddy Wright cranked the motor and left toward home. We bade him farewell, entered the house and relayed the story to Mom, who enjoyed the story as much as we did. For several days, this topic dominated family conversations, until it took its rightful place in the corner of our memories.

Years later, as I recall this episode, I concluded that the lights on Daddy Wright's pickup must have always been on bright when he traveled at night. It seems fitting that this grand old gentleman operated his truck as he lived. He remained positive, patient and understanding throughout his ninety-two years, continually looking at the brighter side of his fellowman, always giving the benefit of doubt. As he passed along the roadways of life, Pony

Wright, the consummate Christian, was always stuck on the high beam.

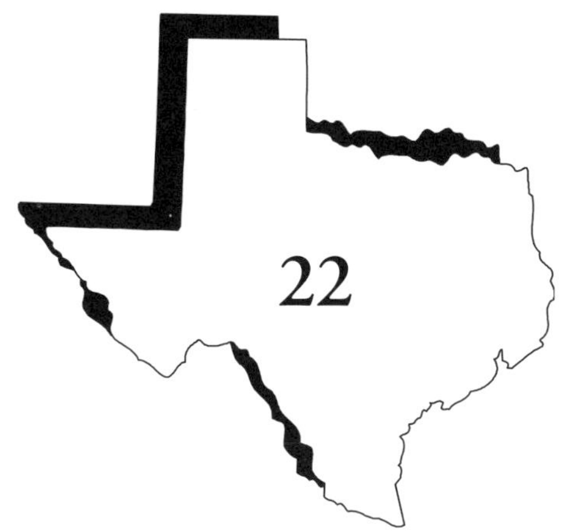

22

THE FISH ANALOGY

AT THE BEGINNING OF THE FIFTH GRADE IN THE fall of 1953, all seemed normal enough, at least according to Chinquapin standards. I sat in the third row in the second classroom and daydreamed, wishing for the day that I would finally move next door to join the bigger folks.

As I mentioned earlier, Chinquapin school had three classrooms. The first one housed the primary and second-year students; the middle contained the third, fourth and fifth grades; and the last held the sixth and seventh grades. After completing the seventh, the pupils transferred to San Augustine, where they continued their education until graduating high school.

At Chinquapin School, the area in which one sat identified one's rank within the system. The first graders—or primers as we called them—were segregated in one row, the second graders in another, and so on. There were two teachers and a principal, who also taught the sixth- and seventh-grade levels.

The three rooms, with no partition walls, were divided only by space between the rows. While the teachers interacted with the members of one grade, they kept the others busy with assignments on different subjects until it came time to move on to another class. Each instructor followed the same format.

That is the way it was day after day. While my teacher taught others, I always tried to finish my assignments as soon as possible so that I could pay more attention to the lessons being dispensed in the upper levels. Most of my classmates did the same thing, soaking up those advanced words of wisdom. In that atmosphere of openness, teachers often presented common material to more than one class at the same time.

On occasion, all students participated in a spelling contest, and it was fairly common for a fourth or fifth grader to beat out one in the sixth and seventh for the grand title of spelling bee champion. As strange as it may seem, it appeared that most of the students who occupied the same homeroom were pretty evenly matched on the achievement scale.

I suppose that in many ways, Chinquapin's educational system seemed archaic, but as I reflect on the matter, we may have attained some of the best successes possible. And as for the teachers, I stand in awe of their unique abilities and devotion. As a former teacher, I will never fully comprehend how they managed to juggle their time in that open-class atmosphere and still make every student in their care feel as if he or she was the most important being on campus.

I will never forget the day that Mrs. Smith, who had taught at Chinquapin for about three years, told five students, including yours truly, to pick up their personal belongings and accompany her next door. She announced that Mr. Emmons, the school principal, wanted to talk to us. We were nervous and completely dumbfounded. The principal never wanted to just talk or pass away time, unless a student got into trouble and needed some close and personal, hands-on attention.

Mann Emmons served as the principal of Chinquapin during that period. My family had known him for quite a while, and in fact, my mother taught him when he was in grade school.

As you can imagine, I feared the worst when Mrs. Smith said, "Come with me!" But when I stopped to consider that the term was still young, I knew that I had not yet had time to become embroiled in another of my so-called episodes. So I decided that Mr. Emmons wanted me to deliver a message to my mother. Perhaps he wanted her to substitute-teach for a few days, a practice that she did often. But what about the other four? What had they done to deserve the principal's attention?

The five of us were unprepared for what followed. When we filed into his room, the principal immediately began talking about class sizes, and other things that flew completely over our heads. Mr. Emmons pointed to us individually. Then he called our names and told us to take our seats at the end of the sixth-grade row. Although complying without so much as a single question, we remained totally baffled. Then, Eunice McDaniel, one of our select group, whispered, "Promotion!"

I dismissed this interpretation entirely. Sure, I knew what the word meant, but at the present, promotion seemed illogical. This was but the beginning of the fifth grade, and we had a lot of ground to cover until the following May, when the real promotion time rolled around. But I had not yet seen the paddle either, so the perception that Mr. Emmons was building toward something sinister began to fade. I sat and waited.

During September 1953, Chinquapin school faced a crisis of sorts. There were too many fifth graders, and the excess spilled over into temporary seating arrangements. Added to that, the sixth-grade row was short by some five students.

Certainly we knew that our fifth-grade class was the largest to come along in quite a while, but we were not privy to all the discussions held in those after-class meetings. Our renowned educators determined that current excess and shortage ratios completely upset the delicate stability of class structure. The ballast shifted, and something had to be done—and quickly—to right the ship.

While searching for a solution to the plight of class imbalance, Mr. Emmons and Mrs. Smith put their heads together and came up with a fantastic idea. What if they promoted five fifth-grade students to the sixth? That would even out the row situations, and at the same time, bring all classes to the desired levels. When Mr. Emmons heard Eunice's faint observation—"Promotion"—he smiled, nodded in agreement and then tried to put it all in perspective. In unmistakable language, we were skipping the fifth grade.

So that is how it came to be. But before we became too familiar with our new-sprung and majestic stations in life, Mr. Emmons diluted the euphoria with notice, emphasizing that one serious barrier remained. This promotion was temporary, and in order for it to become permanent, our parents had to first consent, then issue the final approval in written form. He allowed us but one day to deliver a note from home, because school had been in session for almost two weeks. The new sixth graders had some catching up to do, and he didn't want to lose additional time in getting us up to speed. I determined early on that neither parent would pose a threat and stand in my way, so what could possibly happen? My position was safe, I felt, and tomorrow, I would deliver Mom's glowing endorsement.

Suddenly my head swelled more than three hat sizes, and I seemed to float in air. Most certainly, this represented the biggest win to come my way. Although I shared the educational lottery proceeds with four others, I considered myself the luckiest kid in Chinquapin school history. I concluded that surely this must be a first. Not only had I traveled to new frontiers, I now stood at the pinnacle of success, savoring the fruits of cutting-edge developments. All this was hard to believe, so I pinched myself to make sure that I was not dreaming. *Won't Mom and Dad be proud of me?* I thought. *I can't wait to get home to give them the good news.* But then I remembered that Dad was away from home working on some pipeline.

While I basked in the glory of self-adoration, Mr. Emmons slipped in additional words of warning. "Now if your parents don't consent, I will have no choice but to put you back. If that happens, we'll pick an alternate."

I concentrated on those three telling words: put you back. As for alternate, I had no idea what it meant, but I would ask Mom when I got home. In those days, if I didn't understand something in school, I waited until Mom filled in the missing spaces. That way I would be spared the embarrassment of asking a teacher to repeat something—or worse still, being chastised for not paying attention in class.

Up to that point in my life, I had never experienced such a joyous feeling. I could scarcely contain the excitement. By the time the recess bell rang, we five were now deemed to be the smartest kids in our old class and probably the entire school. Something, however, was amiss. In fact, many of my so-called buddies, with whom I had shared the most vicious storms, now began to look at me differently. Why, I even heard Lee Allen call me a smart aleck. Afterwards, he walked away in disgust. I failed to understand that his feelings were hurt, because he was not chosen to walk among the gods and take his just place in the last five seats of the sixth-grade class.

At home, another unknown skulked in the shadows— one that completed blindsided me. As expected, I bolted into the house to find Mom immersed in preparing the evening meal. I proudly proclaimed that I, at the tender age of ten, had become a sixth grader. I waited for the anticipated praise and admiration that would surely follow. Mom managed but a half-smile and even showed signs of disappointment. In a few minutes, she removed her apron and asked me to sit. She wanted to talk with me a while. I had come to like all this discourse of late, and now Mom was probably going to really show some fine appreciation for my efforts and latest accomplishment. She calmly asked me to describe exactly what I meant.

After I recounted the glorious event of the day, Mom responded with silence. When she resumed the conversation, however, I really did not grasp what she had in mind. She referred to something about class levels being designed to include children that were near the same age. She talked about fish out of water and swimming against the flow. I had not a clue how fish or water related to my recent promotion, but regardless, Mom continued. She spoke of terms such as maturity, likes, dislikes, sharing—and things in common.

She emphasized that I had started school at the age of six, while others began at seven. If I jumped a grade, some of my fellow students would be two years older than I was. She interpreted this age difference as a real hurdle, maybe not so much now, but in the years to follow. I would come to learn that she was right. Some of the girls in my class would be more advanced, and that would upset the applecart and the dating regimen.

"What are you talking about? What's that got to do with anything?"

I'M TOTALLY CONFUSED!

I believed that my appeal deserved special consideration, but Mom had other ideas. With a stern attitude, she said that she would not allow me to stay in the sixth grade—no ifs, ands or buts. I was not yet ready. That's that! I would have to go back. The decision was final! At last, she had spelled it out. Now I understood. What a blow!

"No way," I said, "You can't expect me to do that. Why, I won't be able to show my face in school ever again. I might as well move, leave the country or better yet, quit school altogether."

Is this how one is repaid for such hard work and sacrifice? What would my friends think of me? For hours, I begged and pleaded with the best in the business. If Oscars were given for best performance in pleading, mine would have gained, at the very least, a nomination.

The groveling effort, however, never received honorable mention, and it fell unexpectedly short of its mark. Then I tried sobbing, pouting and everything that I could think of to get Mom to change her mind. I was determined to keep my grand prize, no matter what. But Mom threw aside my best strategy, and I became resigned to failure. That night, I cried myself to sleep. Now before you go calling me a crybaby and a wimp, please realize that this was serious business. I had to save my honor and find a way to snatch victory from the jaws of defeat.

"If only Dad was here," I observed, "he would certainly stand by me. He would tell Mom a thing or two."

The hours of darkness seemed endless, and the restlessness produced very little sleep. When Mom stood at the door of my bedroom the following morning and announced that it was time to get up, I tried to ignore her. When that didn't work, I feigned illness, but Mom saw through that lame excuse. With patience wearing thin, she resorted to the best weapon in her arsenal to spur me on. She threatened, "I'll tell your dad about this when he gets home."

As usual, that did the trick. After quickly placing both feet on the floor, I changed speed and moved at a snail's pace. I hated to confront my classmates, both old and new, but most of all, I had not yet figured out what I would say to Mr. Emmons. I could not deal with the disastrous possibility of walking back into that fifth-grade classroom and having to endure the lingering snickers and innuendoes. This new day would most assuredly bring shame and disgrace to the family name.

Even in the depths of absolute despair, life goes on. I dressed slowly and walked to the breakfast table. To my surprise, however, I found a note in my chair. While sitting down, I opened the folded piece of paper. It read: "Mr. Emmons, Fred Barry has my approval to stay in the sixth grade as long as he can do the work. Signed, Myrtle."

The sweet smell of victory filled my nostrils. Wearing a grandiose grin that extended from ear to ear, I ran to Mom and hugged her neck. I apologized for the way that I had behaved the previous afternoon and night, but I explained that she just didn't understand what I was going through.

She smiled and said, "I only want what is best for you." But as usual, Mom got the last word. She could not help interjecting a parting shot by saying, "Son always be careful of what you wish for, because sometimes you get it."

I brushed aside those pearls of insight as just another anecdote. Then I finished eating, grabbed my books and jumped into the bus with my note in hand. At school, I delivered it to Mr. Emmons who placed it inside his desk drawer, and I took my rightful place in the assigned seat within the sixth-grade row. Only then did I recognize that I had forgotten to ask Mom about that word, alternate.

"I'll find out about it later," I said to myself, but I decided to leave well enough alone. For the time being, I adopted the motto: Let sleeping dogs lie.

As far as the rest of the story is concerned, I adapted quickly to my new surroundings. In fact, I never faced any class-related setbacks until about the eighth and ninth grades when my buddies started dating. Even then, I still enjoyed playing cowboys and Indians and frankly, I could not understand why fellows wanted to hang around a bunch of girls. A couple of years later when I began to figure out that thing called romance, words from the past resurfaced.

Yep, Mom was right, as usual. Most of the girls in my class were at least two years older, and in order for me to date those my own age, I had to step down about two grade levels, where I found many to be quite immature. At the time, I never considered the flip side; perhaps some of the girls in my individual class thought me to be a little wet behind the ears. I was caught in the middle. Could it be that we had nothing in common?

Then I recognized what Mom meant when she offered those prophetic words of bygone days, "Son, if you go into the sixth grade now, you will be like a fish out of water, and in many ways, you will always find yourself swimming upstream and against the current. But go ahead. You will not be happy unless you give it a try."

Over the years, some have questioned how I was able to graduate high school at the youthful age of sixteen. Early on, I used to lay out the story in graphic detail, but after a bit, I learned that few outside my immediate family really cared to hear about one of the great success stories of my life. The last time that I brought it up in a discussion with a friend, he asked for some clarification. Of course if I thought that he held a genuine interest, I would have taken the time to describe the complete event. In order to determine the real motive or whether he was merely being polite, I issued a vague response, "It was all a matter of being in the right place at the right time."

I waited patiently for the next series of questions that never came. My friend never delved further, and after a brief interlude, we began talking about things of far greater importance: the weather and the stock market.

As my thoughts return to this subject, I search for comparisons. Recently I heard an advertisement about South Carolina's Educational Lottery and how easy it is to play and win. That took me back to that September day in 1953 when I unexpectedly won Chinquapin's much-earlier version, with a ticket purchased not with money, but with extraordinary circumstances best described by a military term—logistics.

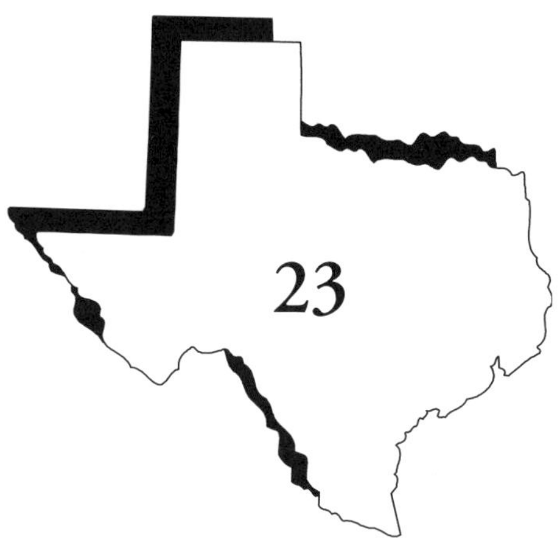

23

THE SMOKEHOUSE EPISODE

THE YEAR OF 1953 REPRESENTED A TURNING point—a defining time that would serve as a crucible from which our true will and character would evolve. Following a previous year's miserable cotton crop that netted just a little more than one bale, Dad decided to stake what was left of our family fortune on a cattle enterprise. So he secured a loan from the Commercial State Bank in San Augustine and used the proceeds to purchase about twenty Brahma heifers from Harlon and Juanita Hall, neighbors of my grandfather Wright. I tagged along on the day that we selected them, and I remember the proud expression on everyone's face as the new recruits were delivered to our place and then released into the pasture.

Preparations had been ongoing for several months. Several additions were made to the property, including a new stock pond located near the lower barn. Dad had planted maize earlier in the season, and as it grew to maturity, the tops swayed in the gentle afternoon breezes. Excitement filled us when we saw that beautiful display and thought about the prospects of a pretty good yield. For the first time in his pursuit of farming, Dad remarked that it looked like everything would fit together.

"Our years of hard work and sacrifice are finally going to pay off," he said. The dividends are close at hand."

We felt blessed indeed, because the temperatures held at a moderate level, while the rains fell at the proper intervals. Things were also going well on other fronts; the Brahma herd prospered and matured quickly. And then, who could ever forget about Joe?

For years we looked forward to the day when he would earn his keep. Dad and I had repaired many a mile of fence damaged by his capers, beginning at the onset of puberty and continuing with the effects of the longstanding squabble with Truitt Henley's Hereford bull. After reflecting on the matter, Dad made another of his epic similes. As usual, this one left me in the dark, at least for the time being. He laughed and remarked, "We have too little fence, and Joe has too much testosterone. That's no even match!"

Now I could relate to the last part of that observation, because that old rascal almost ground me into the dirt years before. With a small amount of descriptive analysis by Dad, however, I began to understand more about that testosterone thing.

When put to the test in the romance department, however, Joe set aside past differences with the neighboring counterpart and looked toward his own pastures. Although he lived up to our expectations and took care of the business at hand when the first opportunity presented itself, his style seemed rather clumsy. In fact it compared favorably with the speed and finesse of a runaway locomotive. But semantics about form and methodology did not bother him, because he was head bull, chief operating executive and financial officer, chairman of the board, president and grand potentate—all rolled into one—who ran the show with unchallenged authority.

When discussing whether Joe's character possessed conceit, arrogance or egotism, all are mere understatements. That old bull strutted among his harem and seemed to say in each of his bellows, "These are *all* mine and I don't have to share them with anybody!"

Just after school started and the weather began to cool somewhat, Dad performed a yearly ritual. He butchered a hog that I called Big Boy and afterward placed the meat in our smokehouse to cure. Right now I'm not sure how familiar you are with smokehouses, but these are generally stand-alone structures, built a good distance from one's house, barn and the like for safety precautions. Green wood, which burned extremely slowly, fed the gentle fire underneath the meat to produce a smoke that would gently cure it, not only to enhance the flavor but also to keep it from spoiling. The addition of salt aided the process; thus the evolution of the term *salt pork.*

Our smokehouse was a little different from most. The lean-to, attached directly to the barn's framework, had been there for as long as I can recall. Each year we prepared and preserved at least one hog without incident, and this season should have been nothing out of the ordinary.

After Dad put Big Boy's carcass on to smoke, he hired a crew to bring in the hay crop. I ran behind the combine and tried to catch rabbits, birds and all types of varmints, flushed out by the noisy activity. *This is a great time to be a kid,* I thought. As a youngster, I placed greater importance on the entertainment value that the project produced than on its actual, more serious purpose. The smell of fresh-cut grain filled my nostrils, and I romped about without a care in the world.

Soon the huge baling machine sat about gathering and tying the anticipated output. Appearing as though they were fallen soldiers strewn about a field of battle, the rectangular bales lay for quite a while in order to dry before we began stacking them in our barn. I wasn't big enough to lift one of those heavy bundles onto the wagon by myself, but just the same, I believed that I had contributed as much as everyone else did. Shortly the hayloft brimmed to capacity.

Dad calculated that the current reserves would carry all of our livestock through the winter. Everything had gone according to plan so far, and by next spring he expected a full complement of calves. He planned to keep the females for future breeding purposes, but the males would be sold to help offset the family's loan obligation. All was good in the McKinley household, but unfortunately things were about to change! I was about to learn what Mom meant when she often said, "What one expects rarely happens—you have to be on the constant lookout for the unexpected."

One Sunday we attended morning services at the Chinquapin Baptist Church, which stood near the crossroads just above Preston Ainsworth's store. The small house of worship accommodated a congregation of about sixty, and on that particular beautiful day, the turnout was unusually large.

During the singing of the second hymn, "The Old Rugged Cross," my uncle Burrell burst through the front door and shouted, "Fred, your barn is on fire!"

The music stopped immediately and a hush fell about the place. In disbelief, Dad jumped to his feet and ran out of the building toward the Ford pickup, followed by Mom and me. I don't remember how fast we drove for those two miles, but time seemed to stand still. Dad kept asking how the fire could have possibly started? Then the explicable hit us at the same time—the smokehouse had something to do with it surely.

When we arrived at the top of the hill and could see below, the barn was completely ablaze. As Dad turned the corner into the front of our house, we saw my mother fly out of the passenger side, hit the pavement and roll a few times before coming to an abrupt stop. She had opened the door of the truck and readied herself for a fast exit, but the plan obviously backfired. Dad stopped just long enough to help her back in. Mom grimaced a bit from the pain, but she assured him that we had more important things to worry about. At the moment, we failed to recognize that she sustained numerous serious cuts and bruises while falling on the recently blacktopped road-bed with exposed gravel.

I'm not sure why we were in such a hurry. There was nothing that we could have done if we arrived sooner. Chinquapin had no fire department, and besides, there was no water within five hundred feet of the fire. By the time someone mentioned the possibility of a bucket bri-gade, it was much too late.

HOT TIMES AT CHINQUAPIN!

As neighbors and friends gathered about to witness the scene, Mom, Dad and I stood by helplessly and watched the flames consume the building. It was much like attending a funeral of a loved one. Soon nothing remained but a pile of smoldering rubble and broken dreams. That barn had held much more than bales of hay. Our future, tied directly to the contents, hung in the balance!

Within an hour or so, all of the onlookers and well-wishers were gone, leaving the three of us to retreat to the house, each asking why this had to happen to us. Dazed, Dad sat down on the back steps. With his head lowered into his hands, he said, "I guess I might have known. It's just not meant to be."

That was the first time that I ever saw my dad cry.

Days later we poked through the smoldering remains and uncovered a handful of farm implements, some cowbells and an anvil, but nothing else could be salvaged. With winter fast approaching, the family faced a harsh question—a reality check. How were we going to feed the cattle? Dad tried to forestall the inevitable by attempting to borrow more money from both banks in San Augustine, but no further credit could be had.

On April 6, 1865, General Robert E. Lee, standing atop a rise at Sayler's Creek, Virginia, looked upon the shabby remnants of his once-proud Confederate legions and declared, "My God, has the army dissolved?" Shortly thereafter, he made the fateful decision to surrender to Union General Ulysses S. Grant at Appomattox Court House. The formal ceremony occurred just three days later. In part, the finality lay in the fact that he could no longer feed and provide for his remaining forces, once believed invincible.

As a student of the American Civil War, I always drew upon this event for similarities to our predicament. Dad realized that all was lost, because without food, the cattle—like General Lee's battle-weary veterans—would certainly perish. But there was another consideration: he no longer possessed the will to fight the elements associated with farming. As the luck of the draw goes, the odds were just too great. The dream would be abandoned; he had to provide for the family.

With the inescapable at hand, Dad loaded up the cattle and sold them at auction. For reasons of pride, we held Joe until the very last. Selling him was almost more than we could bear. Although the old Brahma and I had had our misunderstandings in the past, he had been the first; now fittingly, he represented the last. But Dad's next announcement—the one that left us all with that queasy, empty feeling way down deep in the pit of the stomach region—finally drove home the fact that our lives would be forever altered.

CHINQUA WHERE?

Toward the fall of 1954, Dad said that he was going to Evadale, a little further toward the coast, to check out a new paper mill that was under construction. My uncle, Jess Simmons, had recently secured a wood-supply contract there and he sent word that Dad might find a permanent job. That particular connotation never meant anything to me until much later when I calculated that at the time my father was forty-three years old and he had never held what we called steady employment.

After Dad left, Mom and I were in a state of suspension, but within days we received the awaited letter. Dad had not only been hired, but his pay was something around $4.50 an hour. That afternoon, as we walked to my grandparents' house, we asked ourselves what in the world we would do with all that money? Imagine that—fifty cents shy of $5.00 per hour!

A couple of months later, Dad placed the farm on the market. It sold quickly, but I was not yet ready for the move to the big city, as we called it. I hated to leave my friends with whom I had gone to school from the first to the seventh grade. Naturally, it was an emotional time, but we handled the relocation to Silsbee, a few miles from Dad's new job, as best we could. We still carried the treasured memories, and we could always come back and visit my grandparents.

Over the years as I looked back on the barn-burning incident, I thought it ironic when I learned that Dad had really caused the calamity. Later on, Mom swore to me that she had cautioned him that morning about placing additional wood on the flames. Dad, unfortunately, failed to heed her advice. He had admonished me earlier about smoking near the barn, and I'm sure that this crossed his mind on more than one occasion, most probably in the still of the night when we pause to reflect on our short-comings. Out of respect, though, I never brought up the subject in our conversations—it was much too painful.

Time helped heal the heartbreak associated with the family's loss, and eventually we were able to discuss the affair without tears of sadness. In fact, we found a lot of humor by recalling the details about Mom's sudden de-parture from the truck and her short-term maiden flight. Previously we had prayed for some county official to pave the old dirt road that ran in front of our house. As it turned out, we finally got our wish about two months before Mom's direct contact with the gravel that tore into her skin. But as they say, "That's progress!" In conclusion, we determined that the old adage is true after all: Laughter is the best cure.

Keep your fears to yourself; share your courage with others.

—Robert Louis Stevenson

Epilogue

A New Perspective

After moving from Chinquapin sometime in January 1955, we returned on many occasions. However, the visits became more infrequent following the deaths of my grandparents, and I rarely saw any old acquaintances or classmates after that. I learned in 1993 that Everett Henley died; his mother and father had preceded him by several years. Larry and Dora Wagstaff, Lee Allen Dickerson, Lue Dean Loggins and Hub Christie are now all gone as well.

The home that belonged to Daddy Wright decayed slowly and then completely disappeared; its original location is now obscured by a new growth of timber. Prior to its final demise, however, members of Uncle Paul Wright's family rescued the organ, so long abandoned on the back porch, and restored it to mint condition. My first cousin, Wayne Wright, saved the gun rack and placed it in his own home. I never found out what happened to the Ford undercarriage on which I played as a kid.

CHINQUA WHERE?

Daddy Wright's store deteriorated with the passage of time, and no traces of it exist. The same applies to that of Preston Ainsworth. As far as our farm is concerned, only one barn and the water well remain. New owners moved our house to a location unknown to current family members, and the same thing happened to the one owned by Grandpa McKinley. Hardy Hill, one of the defining features that stands proud within the borders of our former property, looks very different in my adulthood; it appears much less daunting than when I was a kid trudging up the steep incline to fetch buckets of water.

The road between the two general stores that led to the rickety wooden bridge over Chinquapin Creek toward the school has grown over with trees and thick underbrush. The church congregation now meets in a new brick structure, updated with a detached community center. My cousin, Sissy Sharp Fults, purchased the original building and moved it down the road a short distance, where she uses it to house an antique and resale shop—just like the old sanctuary that was converted into the Grand Ole Opry, it lives on. Some of the other area homes occupied by old friends have changed hands, but most have vanished.

The community, as I remember it, has changed dramatically. When I last visited there in May 1999, few recognizable landmarks remained. Newer homes and sur-

rounding buildings had completely changed the landscape. The schoolhouse was torn down long ago, and
the grounds are now part of Chinquapin Cemetery, where
my dad and several generations of family members rest
in peace.

As I drove those back roads, so different from in 1955,
I thought about how sad it is that Americana is being lost.
But I suppose the term *Americana* is relative, as each
generation tends to redefine itself. New experiences are
forged, memories are created and the torch is passed
from one generation to the next, just as it should be.

In that respect I gained a sense of comfort. Chinquapin, all my old friends, relatives—and others including the
pets and farm animals, both living and departed—will
remain the same as long as I remember and write about
them. And I have never—not even for one day—forgotten from whence I came. Perhaps, beyond all others,
these are the only true and lasting lessons.

Appendix

When we came into the world, we knew naught of what had been before us; but as we came to the years of understanding, we learned of the past. We learned what men had thought, and said, and done, from the beginning of the world to our day. But only through the eye of faith and understanding can we behold what is to come hereafter, and only through a firm reliance upon the Divine promises, can we satisfy the yearnings of our immortal souls.

Grand Lodge of Texas, A.F. & A.M.
Monitor of the Lodge

Recommended Reading and Reference List

Books

Clark, Anne. *Historic Homes of San Augustine*. Jointly
published. San Augustine, Texas: The San Augustine
Historical Society, 1972. Austin: Encino Press, 1972.

Ferguson, Ernest B. *Chancellorsville, 1863*. New York:
Alfred A. Knopf, 1992.

Grand Lodge of Texas, A.F. & A.M. *Monitor of the
Lodge*. Waco, Texas: Waco Printing Company, 1982.

McWhiney, Grady, and Jamieson, Perry D. *Attack and
Die: Civil War Military Tactics and the Southern Heri-
tage*. University of Alabama, 1982.

Marler, Don C. *Fort Terán on the Neches River*. Hemphill,
Texas: Dogwood Press, 2000.

Nevin, David. *The Texans: the Old West Series*. New
York: Time-Life Books, 1975.

Proctor, Ben. *Just One Riot: Texas Rangers in the 20th Century*. Austin, Tx: Eakin Press, 1991.

Scurlock, Virgie Worsham. *History of McMahan's Chapel*. No publisher data, 1979.

Sitton, Thad. *The Texas Sheriff: Lord of the County Line*. Norman, Okla.: University of Oklahoma Press, 2000.

Wheeler, Richard. *Witness to Appomattox*. New York: Harper & Row, 1989.

Williams, John Hoyt. *Sam Houston: A Biography of the Father of Texas*. New York: Simon & Schuster, 1993.

Wooster, Ralph. *Lone Star Regiments in Gray*. Austin: Eakin Press, 2002.

————. *Lone Star Generals in Gray*. Austin: Eakin Press, 2000.

————. *Texas and Texans in the Civil War*. Austin: Eakin Press, 1995.

Online Articles

"CHINQUAPIN, TX." The Handbook of Texas Online. http://www.tsha.utexas.edu/handbook/online/articles/view/CC/htc5.html

"CHINQUAPIN CREEK." The Handbook of Texas Online. http://www.tsha.utexas.edu/handbook/online/articles/view/CC/rbcdr.html

Online References

McKinley, Fred B. http://www.chinquawhere.com

Texas Escapes Magazine. http://www.texasescapes.com

Wright, Jerry. http://www.geocities.com/pickinwright/index.htm

Index

Index

A Note about the Author

A descendant of Revolutionary War, War of 1812, War for Texas Independence and Confederate soldiers, and whose father served in the U.S. Navy during World War II, Fred B. McKinley embarked on a long and distinguished career in the credit industry and retired with the Louisiana Department of Justice. A native of Beaumont, Texas, he graduated from Lamar State College of Technology (1964) and Lamar University (1987). He attended Louisiana State University (1995), where he received a law enforcement certification. McKinley, the author of *The Yount-Lee Oil Company* (M.A. thesis, Lamar University, 1987), has also contributed articles to *The Texas Gulf Historical and Biographical Record*, published in Beaumont, Texas; and to the national magazines of *Country* and *Country Extra*, both published by the Reiman Group in Greendale, Wisconsin. He is the father of three children, grandfather of three, and lives in North Myrtle Beach, South Carolina. At the present, he is corroborating with his wife, Dottie, on a historical romance titled *The Celtic Cross.*